Gur Cake & Coal Blocks

This is Éamonn MacThomáis's famous book about growing up and starting to work.

In the days before packaging, Dubliners bought slabs of Gur Cake, burned Coal Blocks sold from a horse and cart, and drank 'loose milk' from the churn and sold sweets and biscuits from large glass jars.

MacThomáis vividly recalls the old electric trams, queueing up with jam jars (as payment) for the fourpenny rush at the cinema, traditional cures and herbs for all ailments — and starting work at 7 a.m. with the horses of the White Heather Laundry.

MacThomáis learned his Dublin street by street delivering laundry — since those days he has studied the history of his city, has lectured and made radio and TV programmes. He has taken many courageous stands for his Republican beliefs, and is an expert on the revolutionary history of Ireland. He is married with four children and lives in Dublin.

'. . . an autobiography by Éamonn, the story of his early life, told with the wonderful attention to detail that illustrates clearly the remarkable memory of the man. For anyone who would like to re-live the irrepressible gaiety of Dublin's war years, this book is a must.'
Paddy Crosbie
The Sunday Press

First published 1976
First paperback edition 1978
Reprinted 1982, 1985, 1988
The O'Brien Press Ltd.
20 Victoria Road, Rathgar, Dublin 6.

ISBN 0-86278-096-9

10 9 8 7 6 5

Éamonn MacThomáis
Drawings Liam Delaney
and Michael O'Brien

Cover Design Michael O'Brien
Layout and Design Michael O'Brien
Typesetting Redsetter Ltd. Dublin
Printed and bound in Great Britain by
The Guernsey Press Co. Ltd.,
Guernsey, Channel Islands.

GUR CAKE
AND
COAL BLOCKS

Éamonn MacThomáis

Illustrated by
Liam Delaney and Michael O'Brien

THE O'BRIEN PRESS
DUBLIN

Contents

Rathmines to Goldenbridge 7

The Kathleen Mavourneen System 15

Dublin Herbs and Cures 21

The Dead Centre of Dublin 27

Lighting the Lamps 34

Pigtown and Basin Lane 39

Schooldays in Richmond Barracks 46

The Magical Brickfields 57

A Volcano at the Hellfire Club 64

Me Proddy Dick Friend 70

The Devil in Inchicore 79

Cockles and Periwinkles 84

A Chiseller's Christmas 90

Gur Cake and Coal Blocks 97

Picking Blackers 103

Grand Canal Playground 109

The Glimmer Man 116

Money in a Tin Box 121

Are you the New Boy? 132

A Lovely Dublin Stew 142

Paying the Rent 150

For my youngest son, Damien

Other books by Éamonn MacThomáis

The Lady at the Gate
Down Dublin Streets 1916
Me Jewel and Darlin' Dublin
The Labour and The Royal
Janey Mack Me Shirt is Black

1

Rathmines to Goldenbridge

I HAVE ONLY a few memories of my birthplace in Rathmines and it was only when we were moving house to Goldenbridge that I became aware of the place. My father, James Heather Thomas, was a month dead and we had to quit the big house in Homeville to make way for the new captain of the Rathmines Fire Brigade.

The furniture van was gone and I remember standing in the hallway of the empty house with a small green vase in my hands. I noticed that the wallpaper was cleaner in those places which had been covered by pictures. At that moment the Rathmines Town Hall clock rang out and I nearly let the vase fall. It was the first and the last time I heard it strike.

Although I don't remember the occasion myself, my mother told a story of the late Captain Whyte who had retired from the Fire Brigade. Apparently the man was in the habit of visiting us once a month. Anyway, when I was three years old, the captain arrived on his usual visit to be met by my sister at the gate.

'Where's your ol' wan?' inquired the captain.

'She's not my ol' wan,' my sister replied. 'She's my mammy.'

The captain then met my brother, asking the same question and getting the same reply. Then the captain met me. I was tied to the pole of the clothes line to keep me off the big fire engine.

7

'Where's your ol' wan?' asked the patient captain again.

'She's up in the kitchen, peeling the spuds,' I replied. So it would appear that I was well versed in the Dublin vernacular at the age of three.

But now I had turned five years of age and I had been instructed by my aunt on the peril of my life, whatever that was, not to drop the green vase. It was of green china with a solid silver band around the mouth of it. My mother had got it as a Christmas present from the jeweller on the Rathmines Road.

My aunt banged the hall door, wiped the tears from her eyes and we set off down to Kelly's Corner to get the tram to Goldenbridge. My aunt was carrying a large pink and gold oil lamp. It was about two foot high and she had it leaning on her shoulder, her two hands being clasped under the circular base.

After what seemed like an hour's waiting the tram arrived. We climbed to the top, which was open to the weather. I took good stock of the tram conductor with his wooden board of coloured tickets. My aunt bought a blue one and told the conductor that I was under-age as regards payment. I was so small that the conductor just nodded, punching one ticket with his silver-coloured machine which sounded like a bell. Overhead, the trolley was hissing along the cable from which came flashes of blue and green.

There were only a few other people on the top and I noticed how they swayed from side to side as the rattling tram moved along the bright rails.

'That's Wellington Barracks,' my aunt said, 'where the Fenian chief, James Stephens, escaped from'.

I looked at the open gate, only one soldier guarding it, and nobody watching the low wall and considered that it was easy to escape from that place. It was, of course, Griffith Barracks, on the South Circular Road but my aunt always referred to places under their old British names, showing her dislike of the same British as she did so.

I was beginning to wonder if my mother, brother and sister had gone off in the furniture van. The tram swayed on its

9

way and the spring breeze was soft on my face and hair. The conductor was calling out the place names of the stops. My aunt paid no attention. I was fascinated by the list of names and wondering when he was going to call out the name of our destination, Goldenbridge; but then I heard Dolphin's Barn announced, saw the tall Celtic cross and asked what that was.

'That's a Penal Cross,' replied my aunt. 'That's where Paddy Pearse spoke for the Volunteers'.

Then she started singing to herself, some words of a song about the Angelus Bell and the Foggy Dew. Half-way through the song she stopped to ask if I were tired or hungry, or was the vase too heavy. But I was too excited to be either tired or hungry and I was enjoying my tram-top ride.

Soon afterwards the tram stopped on the slope of a hill and the conductor climbed the stair to the top and shouted: 'Last stop, Rialto Bridge. Last stop, Rialto Bridge'.

'We have to get off,' said my aunt.

'Where's Goldenbridge?' I asked.

'We will have to walk the rest of the way,' she told me.

We were soon out of the tram and standing on Rialto Bridge. I caught a glimpse of the canal waters, the tall green rushes and a family of snow-white swans, and at that moment fell in love with Rialto Bridge.

'Is this Goldenbridge?' I asked.

'No,' said my aunt. 'It's at the end of the road, around the corner'.

As soon as I saw the long, tree-lined South Circular Road I was tired, hungry and the vase weighed like a ton of bricks. If I fell in love with the Rialto Bridge I hated the S.C.R., it looked so long and the trees made it look longer.

We walked along, my aunt never saying a word except, a few times, to tell me for God's sake to get out from under her feet. When we got to the house on Goldenbridge Avenue, half of the furniture was in the front garden. My grandmother, my mother and my other aunt were trying to sort things out. The linoleum would not fit and would have to be cut. It seemed we had too much furniture and my grandmother said it was a good thing it wasn't raining.

'We are out in the country,' she told my mother. 'How are we going to survive? It's so far from Dublin, I'd never be able to walk it, that's for sure'.

We were ordered out to play and make sure we did not wander too far from the house or else we would be lost. I remember walking down to Suir Pond. There was a wide clay bank on one side of it and a small wall which led to the farm and orchard gardens of the Little Sisters of the Poor: St. Patrick's Home. We looked over the wall and saw a few nuns saying their prayers and a few lambs eating grass.

At the end of the clay bank a lane led to Anderson's Bus Depot. But we only looked down the lane and ran home when we saw a big bus coming up. The next thing we explored was our house and garden.

'Glory be to God,' said my mother. 'How are we going to cut the grass? '

It was nearly as high as the hall door, in a big corner house garden full of weeds, dock leaves and yellow flowers which we learned later were called 'Piss-in-the-beds,' and thousands of fluffy white 'Jinny Joes'.

The back garden was very small. It was no more than a small yard with no grass or weeds. The previous owner of the house had had it covered with red cement. The toilet was in the back-yard beside a door which led to a small kitchen which we called a scullery; the bath and the boiler were in that scullery. It led to a parlour which was a fair-sized room with a small coal-house and gas meter off it in a room of its own; this room became known as the 'mine'. It was really a small cupboard under the stairs.

The halldoor was beside the stairs which led to three bedrooms. It was a Corporation house which we would own in 40 years or 'when I'm pushing up the daisies,' as my mother would say.

All the downstairs floors were made of red cement as the previous owner had had an aversion to mice. These floors, when polished with 'Cardinal Red,' looked like a palace. They were cool in summer and warm in winter and we never

11

had to worry about woodrot.

The fire was a black range which you would have to sit on to get a heat. My aunt spent nearly half the day cleaning and polishing it with 'Zebra' black-lead. Beside the range, in a corner, stood the cabinet-type gramophone of solid mahogany, home-made by my uncle who was a carpenter with Brooks Thomas & Co., Ltd. We had a large collection of records and every Sunday night we took turns at turning the handle to play all my mother's favourites: Down by the Old Bull and Bush , Sweet Nellie Deane , The Desert Song , John McCormack singing the Snowy Breasted Pearl , and Richard Tauber... Jimmy O'Dea..... Kathleen Mavourneen.

I nearly knew them backwards. With no radio or TV in those days the winter evenings were spent around the range with the gramophone or a book. Sometimes the night was spent reading the newspaper. The death notices always were read first and if any friends or relatives were announced dead, the story of their lives was told.

My mother never could see bad in anyone and when my aunt would say that someone was a drunkard, my mother would reply: 'Ah, sure, God love him, Mary, he had his own troubles. Only God knows what he was suffering'.

The first golden rules of life I learned from my mother: never tell a lie, even if it's to save your life; never steal anything or take what belongs to another; never refuse a poor man a penny; never do a bad turn on anyone; when you are in trouble always say 'Sacred Heart of Jesus I place all my trust in thee'.

These are my first memories of Rathmines and Goldenbridge. We were only a few days in the new house when I learned my first song, 'The Tri-coloured Ribbon O', written by the late Peadar Kearney who also wrote the National Anthem, 'Amhran na bhFiann', and several other popular songs. My mother was getting me ready for bed at the time. I was sitting on the bed with my head in her lap. She fondled my hair and then started singing.

I went asleep with the chorus in my ears... 'All around my hat I'll wear a tri-coloured ribbon o'... and the next day I

THE THREE-COLOURED RIBBON

Peadar Kearney

To Eva

I had a true love, if ever a girl had one
I had a true love a brave lad was he,
And one fine Easter Monday, with his gallant comrades,
He started away for to make Ireland free.

Chorus:

So all around my hat I wear a three-coloured ribbon,
All round my hat until death comes to me,
And if anybody's asking why I'm wearing that ribbon,
It's all for my true love I ne'er more shall see.

He whispered, "Good-bye love, old Ireland is calling,
High over Dublin our Tri-colour flies,
In the streets of the City the foe man is falling,
And wee birds are singing 'Old Ireland arise'."

His bandolier around him, his bright bayonet shining,
His short service rifle, a beauty to see,
There was joy in his eyes, though he left me repining,
And started away for to make Ireland free.

In prayer and in watching the dark days passed over,
The roar of the guns brought no message to me.
I prayed for Old Ireland, I prayed for my true love,
That he might be safe, and Old Ireland be free.

The struggle has ended, they brought me the story,
The last whispered message he sent unto me,
"I was true to my land, love; I fought for her glory,
And gave up my life for to make Ireland free."

13

watched the women's hats to see if any of them was wearing such a ribbon, orange, white and green. But I didn't see any, not even down at Kilmainham Cross, where the trams passed, so I became convinced that my mother was the only woman in the world who wore a tri-coloured ribbon on her hat.

Within a few months my name was called to attend school in Goldenbridge Convent. I bawled all the way up to school, during school and ran home at lunch hour and said I was never going back to school again. I must have kicked up a terrible fuss because I was kept at home for a few weeks and then my mother told me she was bringing me to a new lovely school in Basin Lane.

The next day we got the tram to James's Street and walked up to Basin Lane Convent where I fell in love with Sister Monica. My first classroom was known as the 'tram' but, as the days wore on, that was the only tram I had as I had to walk up and down to school to save the penny tram-fare for a poor man. And, besides, I now had to buy school-books and black babies. The schoolbooks would be no trouble at all, as I had a nice little school bag for them. But where was I going to put the black babies?

2

The Kathleen Mavourneen System

THE BEAUTIFUL SONG, 'Kathleen Mavourneen', which was very popular in my childhood days, contained the lines: 'It may be for years and it may be forever'. Dublin wits were quick on the job, and anything bought on a weekly instalment plan basis became known as the Kathleen Mavourneen system.

In the early 1930s salesmen, mainly Jewish, went from door to door selling all kinds of things. Their rates varied from sixpence a week to a half-crown a week. During the Eucharistic Congress in 1932 they had a field day: Holy pictures of St. Patrick casting out the snakes; the Holy Father in Rome; saints of every nation; statues in glass shades; and even a large book containing the 14 Stations of the Cross. This book was published by Clery's of O'Connell Street long before the late Denis Guiney took over.

The first time I became aware of the system was the day the traveller called with a holy picture under one arm and a yellow canary, in a cage, under the other. The yellow bird was singing and I was fascinated by it. The Granny was taking the picture which to-day hangs in my bedroom. It depicts a Mass scene with Christ hanging from the cross down over the altar, a very impressive picture, with the hand of the priest raised and the altar boy ringing the bell.

The Granny was undecided about the canary. The traveller, having made one sale, was pushing to make another.

'But Madam, it's a beautiful bird and it would look so well on top of your gramophone. Listen to the music of his songs'.

'True for yeh, Mister', I said to myself, 'it's a smashing singer'.

'No', said the Granny. 'I won't take it'.

'But Madam, it's only sixpence a week'.

'No, no' the Granny said again. 'I won't take it'.

The traveller tried again.

'But, Madam, for you only, I'll let you have it for three-pence a week and I'll take a shilling off the full price'.

The Granny's voice became angry: 'No, no, no. Take it out of here. Go on, now, take it out of here'.

The traveller was shocked at this sudden change in Granny's voice. His face changed. He was unsure of himself. He remained silent for a few moments thinking, I suppose, that Granny was going to give him back the holy picture as well.

Then the Granny spoke again: 'No' she said, 'and it's kind of you to reduce the price for me. I'll take the picture but get that bird out of here'.

The traveller smiled, regained his own confidence and said: 'Very well, Madam'.

As he was about to leave he smiled and asked: 'What made you change your mind about the bird?'...

The Granny's voice was now soft and sad.

'I'll tell you why', she said, 'because every time I'd look at that bird fluttering his wings against the cage, I'd see the Fenian prisoners grabbing the iron bars in English dungeons'.

The traveller left quickly and Granny went up the stairs to her bedroom to hang up the picture over her bed and have a little weep for the Fenians. As she climbed the stairs she sang out loud:

'Tis 50 long years since I saw the moon beaming
on brave manly forms, on eyes with hope gleaming.
I see them again. Oh it's all my sad dreaming.
Glory O, Glory O, to the bold Fenian men.'

The small man with the brown leather attache case started

selling shoe laces from door to door and he, too, gave credit. Soon he added pins and needles to his trade and later appeared with a larger, brown attache case. Now he sold darning wool and balls of blue which, he claimed, made clothes bright and clean.

I suppose the electric light and gas meter will always remain on the 'never-never' system. When our light went out and we hadn't a shilling for the meter we lit up a few half-penny candles. The old candle holders which were like a large plate with a handle were also sold on the 'never-never'.

The gas meter was only a penny a go and it was fascinating to watch the gas-man empty the meter and count the mountain of pennies into tall towers, his hand working like magic. They were the quickest counters of money that I ever saw. They always gave a refund which came in handy to buy something extra for the dinner.

The gas-men carried the old doctor's type bag and the Gas Company van drove around after them, using a strange-sounding horn to let the collectors know what road the van was on.

'Put it on the slate, please' was still being used when the shopkeepers no longer had chalk and slates, but fancy pencils and account books.

Two institutions the Granny and Ma always avoided were money-lenders and Providence clothing cheques.

When the 'never-never' became known as 'hire-purchase', one of the best firms in Dublin to deal with was McHugh Himself, in Talbot Street. That's where I got my first bicycle at half-a-crown a week during my laundry days.

The people also organised a system of 'clubs', which, in a way, were the forerunners of the Credit Unions of to-day. You drew a number in the club and when your number came up, you went that week and purchased your article in the shop.

Lavin's Stores, beside the Black Lion in Inchicore, was the best value in Dublin for club-holders.

Coal clubs also were organised but, when we could not afford even a half-crown a week for the coal club, I was sent to Keogh Square for a stone of coal for four-pence-ha'penny and a stone of logs for two-pence-ha'penny. With Dick's free turf we managed firing for the week.

Our fire was never lit until 5 p.m. in the evening so that we could save coal. It was lit at that time to have the room warm for Ma when she returned from work.

The last 'never-never' as a child was my first suit of long trousers:

'Ding dong, ding dong,
Eamonn's got his longers on'

'Hey, who lifted you into them?' These were some of the comments when I appeared in my blue serge suit. The woman opposite had told Ma that I could get a new suit at a half-crown a week. The tailor was from Heytesbury Street. The suit was made. Ma was very pleased. I looked like Little Lord Fauntleroy.

The following Friday the tailor came to issue his collection card and collect his half-crown. Ma nearly died when she saw the price of the suit: £7.17s.6d.

'Glory be to God' she said. 'They are only £2 in Guiney's, if we had the money'.

This was during the days when Dublin had its fill of Fifty Shilling tailor shops. We paid and we paid and we paid. We were still paying long after the suit had become thread-bare and shiny. One night we counted up the payments and found, to our delight, that we owed only five shillings.

Ma decided we'd give the tailor the five bob on the Friday and be rid of him forever. When Friday came the tailor informed Ma and me that the suit wasn't fully paid: we still owed another two pounds.

The tailor, Ma and I totted up the card again and it came to seven pounds, seventeen shillings and sixpence.

'That's right', the tailor agreed, 'but the price of the suit is £9.17s.6d.'.

It transpired that the 'nine' was written quickly and it looked more like a seven. The next 16 weeks to clear the £2 were the longest in my life. When the last half-crown was paid the 'never-never' ended forever at our hall-door.

19

3

Dublin Herbs and Cures

I THINK ME Ma and me Granny should have been medical doctors. It's true, they had a cure for almost everything. The Granny said: everyone has to eat a bag of dirt before they die, while Ma's favourite saying was, 'An apple a day keeps the doctor away'.

Now the only time I saw apples was when we boxed the fox or collected them door-to-door on a Hallowe'en evening. The only time we saw the doctor was when we were very ill and the homemade cures and herbs were not sufficient. When the Granny or the Ma said, 'I don't like the look of him, we'd better send for Doctor Power. How much does he charge? A half-a-crown a visit. We'll manage somehow. I don't like the look of him', and down she'd go for old Doctor Power.

A bedside vigil would be kept till the doctor arrived. 'How do you feel', the doctor would ask: 'stick out your tongue, say ah, say ah, and then breathe in and out' as his cold steel disc went up and down my chest or back. The old doctor was a gentleman and I always thought that he could tell more by just looking at me than by using his wooden stick for my tongue and his steel disc for my chest. I never once heard him say what was wrong with me, as that was always whispered to the Ma outside the bedroom door, but I never failed to hear his remedy — M. & B. tablets, and quinine and iron, and see that he doesn't let the quinine and iron near his teeth. Sure the sound of that would nearly cure me! The medicine had a taste that a stone of sugar would not remove. But as I said, the doctor's visits were few and so the homemade cures kept me alive.

For sore eyes or a blast, it was cold tea bathed on the eyelids and it never failed to do the job. A lump or a bump on the head was always treated with a cold saucer or iron and the lumps vanished away. Nose bleeding was treated by a wet cloth on the back of the neck, and cuts of any kind got a dark brown stain of iodine, which stung like hell, smelled like hell and it would take nearly a month before the stain wore off. But again it always did the job. A burn or a scald always brought forth the soap which was rubbed and rubbed until the pain ceased — white Sunlight soap or red carbolic soap dipped in water and applied to the wound. Unlike the iodine, the soap had a lovely smell, not a perfume smell, but a smell of cleanliness which as the advertisement said 'made you feel rosy all over' — but when some people took a double meaning out of that saying, the advertisement disappeared.

Soft green soap was always used for skin rashes and pimples. It was sold in chemist's shops only and came out of a large glass jar, sold by the ounce, if I remember right, it was used mainly for washing hair. It was like ointment in appearance and was packed in wooden tubs. The chemist used a large wooden spoon and filled the wooden tub, like the way ice-cream tubs were filled.

A sprained wrist was usually bound by the skin of an eel, a dock leaf was applied to a nettle sting and a rub of a ball of blue for the sting of a wasp. Warts were treated by your fasting spit and the sign of the cross—try it as soon as you waken in the morning: wet your finger with spittle, run it on the wart, making the sign of the cross, and in due course the warts will disappear. Chilblains, which attacked our feet in winter-time, were dipped in your own urine — I often felt foolish with my two feet stuck in the chamber pot, but to remove that terrible pain and itch I'd have put my feet anywhere. An old night watch-man told me that he treated his piles by sitting on a bucket of cow dung. But one had to be very careful as there was a danger of sticking to the bucket.

22

Another man told me that he had an operation to have his piles removed. 'Well', he said, 'the pain I suffered. I declare to God I'd rather have me piles back'.

Boils, which usually broke out on the back of my neck, or on the leg, were treated with bread and water poultice – a large lump of a fresh loaf steeped in scalding water and applied to the boil. My roars would be heard in Wexford, but the poultice never failed to draw out the poison and the yellow matter, and the boil cleared up within days. Before the poultice was applied I was always warned, 'It's either this or get it cut off with a knife'. With a choice like that I wasn't even fit to revolt.

Blackheads on the face were removed with hot towels or holding your face over a basin of boiling water and letting the steam draw them out. Corns were removed with an open razor and I often wondered how Granny or the Ma didn't remove their toes as well.

Teeth were cleaned with soot and we always had a large supply up the chimney. A toothache or a bad tooth led one to the 'Dental' in Lincoln Place where you could have it removed for a shilling – a real dentist cost a half-a-crown or three shillings. In the 'Dental' the student dentists were trained, and I'm thinking now, it's they that should have given us the shilling. Some of them nearly pulled our heads off. All sorts of toothache cures were available – tinctures, powders and pastes: but in the end, after a few sleepless nights a journey was made to Lincoln Place.

A sore throat was treated by a ladies silk stocking filled with hot salt and tied around the neck. For coughs there were a million cures from lemon drops, black cough bars, bull's eyes sweets, Zubes, Veno's, Sure Shield lozenges, California Syrup of Figs, St. Anthony's cough cure or the smell of hot tar. For the common cold it was a hot bitter lemon drink, and like the man with the piles, I'd rather have my cold any day than drink that terrible stuff!

Hot Bovril or beef tea were the real favourites, with a little Vick rubbed on the chest. If disease came from flies, fleas, bugs, spiders, ear-wigs or black clocks (cockroaches), they were stopped in their tracks by Keating's Powder. 'Keating's Kills' was the slogan — it was the popular method before the birth of D.D.T. and all the other fancy sprays that came later.

Our eyes were protected from the summer sun by green celluloid shields — like those worn by the American newspaper editors or the fellow dealing cards or controlling the roulette table in the Las Vegas casinos. Special prayer-books were printed in very large type for people with weak eyesight; magnifying glasses (the Sherlock Holmes type) were very popular with the older people. A pair of reading glasses could be bought in Woolworths for a few shillings. 'Woolers' also sold cough candy which was very popular with Dubliners. The late John Count McCormack, one of the world's greatest tenors always ate fudge to keep his throat in order. Fudge was very expensive then, and was sold only by Nobletts, the swanky sweet shop in Grafton Street.

A large piece of red flannel was always kept handy for keeping 'the heat in' on lumbago or other aches and pains. A penny poor-man's plaster was also used to 'keep the heat in'. The only trouble with the plaster was taking it off — for it took hair and skin away as it was dragged off.

Mushatt's chemist shop in Francis Street, and The Lucky Man (Nagles) in Meath Street had the greatest collection of cures and herbs in Dublin. Old Mr. Mushatt himself made up thousands of cures, while Mr. Nagle specialised in Poor Man's Plasters and St. Anthony's cough cure. 'Keep the heat in and you'll never be sick'. I was helping an old blind man across the road one day and he told me always to wear me long johns as soon as the cold days appeared and confessed that he put black sugar bags under his long johns and always kept a sheet of brown paper across his chest to keep the wind out and keep the heat in — 'Don't cast a clout 'till May be out'; 'I'm telling you,' he said, 'if you take my tip you'll never be sick — I'm nearly eighty now, but I kept the heat in all me life'. Well, I suppose children didn't need heat; as the Granny always said, 'Young blood should never be cold,' and seemed more concerned with the rain. Wet hair and wet feet were to be avoided at all costs. Wet hair will give you sore eyes and wet feet will give you your end (death). So on a wet day a piece of cardboard was stuck into my boots to prevent the wet getting in by the broken and holed soles. The cardboard wouldn't last long and soon my toes would be swimming around in my wet boots.

Week-in, week-out, whether I needed it or not, I got my dose for the bowels — first it was castor oil, then Epsom's salts or fruit laxatives, and every Saturday night I rebelled. After one serious revolt the leather belt swung in all directions and the dose stopped. A few weeks later I noticed that my Sunday morning tea tasted strange — it also had a strange colour, brown and green. The Ma always said, 'ah it must be stewed, I left it on the gas too long'. Well that was accepted, until I saw the strange green leaves at the end of the cup and discovered it was Senna Pods... another bloody dose: another revolt and the dose stopped. Now I didn't get many sweets in those days, so when I was given a large piece of chocolate and the Ma said I could eat it all myself I thought it was my birthday! Week after week a large piece of chocolate every Saturday night until the night Ma forgot to hide the chocolate box. The name on the box nearly gave me a heart attack — 'Brooklax'. Now if it had of been just 'Brook' it might have been okay, but the word 'lax' could only mean one thing — a laxative — another bloody dose! From that night onwards the chocolate tasted terrible and soon another revolt started. A truce was reached — one small Beecham's Pill swallowed quickly with a cup of real tea solved the problem of the weekly dose.

You know I had great respect for the people who made Epsom Salts and fruit laxatives — like they didn't go behind the door with their products. A dose was a dose and they made no bones about it. But the other people, who tried to pass off their dose as tea or chocolate.... now, I ask you, can you trust anyone?

4

The Dead Centre of Dublin

WHERE'S THE dead centre of Dublin? Corkscrew Alley (Nelson's Pillar)? No. O'Connell Street or the Liffey at Butt Bridge? No. Di ya give up, di ya? Yeh, we give up. Well the dead centre of Dublin is Glasnevin Cemetery. Winter or summer, once a month we visited the father's grave in the dead centre of Dublin. We always seemed to arrive at the gate ten minutes before closing time.

The first thing I saw as we entered the gate was the large black notice board which told in big bold letters and figures "closing time 4 p.m. Sunday". The next thing I saw was the black and gold clock over the office and the gateman's house and its gold hands told the tale: ten minutes to the hour. To make double sure that we saw it, the gateman pointed it out and informed us, 'Yis have only ten minutes. Remember now, ten minutes or yis'll be locked in'. The Ma and the aunt would ignore him but I was always scared stiff. Only ten minutes, sure it would take us nearly twice that long to reach the father's grave in St. Patrick's plot at the far end of the cemetery. I suppose it would not have been too bad if that was the only grave we were visiting but the Ma was really on a tour of the place. After the usual cleaning of the glass shade wreaths, the pulling of high grass and weeds and the decade of the Rosary at the father's grave, we then set off for St. Brigid's plot to visit the Granny's grave, which also got the same attention.

To the memory of
ANNE DEVLIN CAMPBELL
the faithful servant of
ROBERT EMMET
who possessed some rare
and noble qualities
who lived in obscurity
and poverty and so died
on the 18th of September 1851
Age 70 years.
May she Rest in Peace.

Next it was a visit to Matt Talbot's grave, where instead of praying, the mother spoke to him, like as if he was listening to her and we always left the grave with the Ma's words, 'Don't forget now Matt, I'm depending on you'. Next on the tour was Parnell's grave. 'Poor Parnell', the Ma would say, 'he wasn't one of ours, but a few Hail Mary's won't hurt him. Sure he's in heaven, a shining light, the uncrowned King of Ireland'. All this had me very confused – he couldn't be very poor and he in a big grave nearly 100 times bigger than the father's, the granny's or Matt Talbot's. And if he wasn't one of ours, what was he doing here and he must have died before the people got time to crown him King.

The next grave was Anne Devlin's. At the age of ten years I knew the inscription on the tombstone off by heart. 'Ah! God love her', the Ma would say. 'She suffered something terrible'. Between these graves the Ma and aunt would stop at other graves, read the tombstones and tell each other all they knew about the grave and the family who owned it. 'You know them, Sarah', the Ma would say, 'one of them was in the Citizen Army. I think they had a shop on the North Strand; the other brother went with the Free State'.

We then walked around the Republican Plot and again the story would be told of the names on the small slabs of stone. The tour ended at the cross erected to the Manchester Martyrs. 'Some of them were only boys' the Ma would say, and I often noticed tears in her eyes. On our way to the gate a short stop was made at Collins' grave and now the tears would roll down the Ma's cheeks. 'The Treaty' she'd say, 'it ruined everything. That old Lloyd George of England fooled them'. By the time we got to the gate it was nearly five-thirty, the gates were locked.

We seemed to be the only ones in the graveyard now and I was really scared – 'We're locked in – we're locked in', I'd roar as I looked at the high gate and high railings. With a bit of luck I'd be able to climb over, but how in the name of God would I be able to get the Ma and the aunt over it. The aunt always went to the gatekeeper's lodge to ask him to kindly open the gate and let us out. The gatekeeper always came out, with a cup of tea in one hand, a cut of bread in the other, and the ring of large keys hanging from his wrist. He muttered a few curses, told us we were ruining his tea. We waited until he finished eating the cut of bread and drinking a few mouthfuls of tea, muttered to himself a few more curses and warned that the next time he'd leave us locked in for the night.

Sure, God love the poor gatekeeper, we must have had his heart broken for it was the same on every visit, even when the graveyard closed at 5 p.m., we never got to the gate till 6 p.m. I'm sure the Ma and the aunt knew every grave in Glasnevin cemetery — I was always disappointed that they didn't visit the big swanky tombstones on the graves of bishops, lords, ladies, etc., but the tour never varied, except when I insisted on visiting the vaults under the O'Connell tower. When I asked why some of the vaults were locked, the Ma said that some people were buried with their jewels, gold rings and watches, but the aunt insisted that the locks were put on to keep out the body-snatchers. From that day on whenever I saw an old man on his own at a grave I was sure he was a body-snatcher.

The bell that rang at closing time was the loneliest bell I ever heard. It was more like the sound of someone hitting a bucket with a hammer, but later this old bell disappeared and instead the grave-diggers went around ringing bells, like the ones we had in school.

Once in the wet weather the father's grave sank about two foot and we spent all our time that Sunday filling it up with new clay which we carried in Ma's hat and my school cap. One by one the glass shades broke and soon the seven wreaths in the shape of a cross were reduced to bits of glass, broken stone flowers, birds, angels and ribbons. The silver wire surround buckled and the black paint faded on the tombstone, and when the grave sank again the tombstone fell down. We couldn't afford perpetual care, so the Ma slipped the gravedigger a few bob and he said that he'd fix the tombstone, take the buckle out of the wire surround and keep an odd eye on the grave. That was the only day I remember the

Ma crying at my father's grave. I was really delighted when they moved Matt Talbot's coffin to the vaults in the O'Connell tower circle. Now a visit to those vaults was a *must* for Ma — I often looked into the other vaults but I never saw any jewels or gold, but I'm sure I saw plenty of body-snatchers even if I didn't know what they were.

On one occasion the gatekeeper told us that the other gate, Prospect Gate was open and if we liked we could go out by that exit. It wasn't often that this gate was open, but we used it three or four times. Just outside the gate was The Dead-man's Publichouse and of course, I was convinced that it was used by the dead people in Glasnevin Cemetery, with the exception of Parnell and Matt Talbot, because Parnell wasn't one of ours, and the Ma said that Matt Talbot gave up the drink.

Just outside the main gate entrance, the dealers sold flowers and at Christmas-time they sold holly-and-ivy wreaths. My one ambition was to carry a bunch of flowers or a holly-and-ivy wreath to my father's grave. But we never bought any flowers or wreaths—we hadn't the money for such things. In fact the reason we were always late going in to the cemetery was because we were after walking from the Quays at Church Street to save bus fare. It's a fair walk from Church Street Bridge up past the Broadstone, Doyle's Corner, Phibsborough Road, Hart's Corner and the road to the ceme-tery gates. To me as a child, it was the longest walk in the world. Apart from the Deadman's Pub, only three other things seemed to attract me on the journey to and from Glasnevin. The first thing which stuck in my mind was the Brian Boru public house with the large painting of King Brian on his horse holding a crucifix above his head as he led his army into battle the second thing was St. Vincent's Orphan-age, where I was often told I'd end up if I wasn't a good boy.

The third and final thing which never left my mind was the old man lying against the wall of Glasnevin Cemetery. He was a cripple and had a pair of wooden crutches lying beside him on the footpath. I was always given a penny to place in his greasy, dirty cap.

The Ma said he suffered from lead poisoning which scared the life out of me, because I was always biting and chewing the ends of my school pencils and I was sure that I'd end up beside him some day. I often wondered why he chose to lie outside the cemetery wall — and when the Sunday came and he was no longer there, I knew he was now lying the other side of the wall, in Glasnevin Cemetery — the dead centre of Dublin.

5

Lighting the Lamps

THE FIRST TIME I ever heard about lighting the lamps was from me ma. She was telling us the story of how my father got the job as Chief in Rathmines Fire Brigade. 'He did an examination for it,' she said, 'and I lit a lamp for him in John's Lane. I've great faith in lighting the lamps. And he got the job, too,' she added.

'But, sure God love him, he was dead within a year. He was only 31 years old when he died'.

Well, for a long time I wondered where was John's Lane and how did she light the lamps? I wondered did the old lamplighter with the long pole give her a hand, or did she do it all by herself? Also, I didn't know that the street lamps were lit in prayer to God. I thought they were lit to light up the dark streets and lanes in old Kilmainham.

I was six years of age and I was in the Holy Communion class, but Sister Monica in Basin Lane Convent hadn't got around to telling us about lighting the street lamps. Candles was as far as the Sister had got, and about your Guardian Angel standing at your right shoulder. I nearly had a creak in me neck, trying to spot the angel on guard, but as Sister Monica said, he was a spirit, which led to further confusion, when later I read a sign, 'Wines and Spirits' on a shop window – oh I was confused alright.

I decided I'd have a go at lighting the lamps myself, so I waited each evening at the foot of Mount Brown Hill, for

michael O'Brien '72

35

the little man with a black bowler hat and a black coat which nearly touched the ground. The coat was so long, that it was hard to tell whether he was wearing boots or shoes. He smoked an expensive type white clay pipe which had a silver cap on it. The smoke came out of little holes in the silver cap as he puffed and puffed. He also carried a long thin pole with a little flame or the red of a cigarette but at one end. He balanced the pole under his right arm, the centre of the pole resting where his hand was stuck in his pocket; the left hand lifted the clay pipe now and again to allow him to spit in the gutter. Oh I had him well taped and well watched and even followed him a few times without him knowing it, before I worked up courage to ask him about lighting the lamps.

I knew Friday was the best night. It was his pay day, and he seemed to look a bit happier on a Friday. I also noticed that he went in for a few drinks to Muldowney's pub on a Friday. When he came out the pub door, he shook himself, checked his pole, lit his pipe and made his way for the next lamp to be lit. The lamp stood at Kerin's Place. I waited until he was under the lamp post giving the globe and gas jet a look and a nod, then I moved in.

'Mister, Mister Lamplighter, let's have a go Mister — ah go wan Mister, let's light the lamp'.

He never even looked at me. He acted as if I wasn't there. He gave the lamp another nod, and up went the pole as his hand left his pocket and before your could say 'Jack Robinson' the lamp was lit, and blue green and yellow light blinded me eyes. I looked around and the Lamplighter was gone, vanished. I didn't know whether to run up Kilmainham or go around the dark corner in Kerin's Place. Within seconds of the corner being lit up I ran like the hammers of hell.

'Mister, Mister, let's light the next one, Mister'.

But yet again I was left unnoticed. I was about to let out one final roar, when he turned to me and said, 'That's the last wan and thank God me job is done I'll now go home and git me tay'.

He then counted on his fingers — 'Yes,' he said, 'me job is done — Mount Brown one, Watery Lane two, Mountshannon three, Old Kilmainham four, Kerin's Place five, good night me son'.

'Ah Mister, ye didn't let us light any lamps, will ye let's light a few tomorrow night?'

'Oh I couldn't do that' he said, 'I'd be sacked if I did'.

'Well me mother lit them' I said, 'and she said nothing about the Lamplighter being sacked'.

'Did she now' said he, 'isn't she a great woman to be able to light them lamps. It's a work of art ye know, takes years of training, a wrong touch of the pole now, would burst that glass globe. Ye didn't know that, did ye? Oh a work of art, be dad it is. a work of art. I'll tell ye what,' he added, 'if ye meet me here at twelve midnight I'll let ye put out a few lamps. Ye see ye put them out with that' he said, pointing to another part of the pole. 'Go wan home now and tell your mother to bring you down here at midnight tonight'.

I went home disgusted. 'Who the hell wants to put out lamps. It's lighting them that I want to be doing!'

In a way I even envied the altar boys as they went around the high altars in St. Michael's Church, Emmet Road, lighting the big candles. I was sure I could do the job just as good, maybe better than the altar boys, but then I didn't know any Latin. Oh I'd be able to ring the bells at Mass or carry up the water, wine and little white cloth on me arm or even change the Mass book from one side of the altar to the other, and I'd even be able to swing that yoke which filled the church with nice smelling smoke at Benediction, but I'd be caught on the Latin.

Besides, altar boys were considered by us (our gang) to be cissies or snobs, even if they did make a fortune at weddings. Me pal Whacker said that the altar boys got a grush of money all to themselves. Still, I'd have given me right arm to be able to light them big candles.

A few years later I learned from me mother that in John's Lane Church, at the shrine of Our Lady of Good Counsel, instead of lighting candles, people lit little lamps.

Beside the shrine in the Augustinian Church known to Dubliners as John's Lane, Thomas Street, are a couple of glass cases filled with jewellery, watches, rings etc., which were donated by grateful people whose requests and prayers were answered in return for the lamps they lit at the shrine. I'm sure if Fr. E. A. Shelley, O.S.A. were alive today, he would smile at the watches in the glass cases, because the picture frame of Our Lady of Good Counsel in the shrine was purchased by Fr. Shelley for £70 in 1898. The money was raised by a raffle. The first prize was Fr. Shelley's silver watch.

As me childhood days went by I got the chance to light many's the lamp. The nightwatchmen at the road works did not consider it a work of art to light the red warning lamps each evening and they were only too glad to get a few chisellers like meself to help with lighting the lamps. Some were so thankful that an invitation was offered to come and sit in the watchman's hut beside the hot coke fire and enjoy a drop of tay in a tin can and a bit of toast. Not only did we light the lamps, but we cleaned, polished, re-wicked, and refuelled them as well. And after our evening task we would stand back, count them, admire them, watch them flicker and rush quickly to any lamp which seemed to darken rather than glow brightly in the night.

The next morning on the way to school we would notice all the lamps piled in a heap outside the watchman's hut, devil a lamp lighting. All seemed dead and ugly, like the cold cinders in the watchman's fire. We never knew whether it was the watchman or the workmen who put out the lamps, and besides, we didn't worry too much — who the hell wants to put out lights?

6

Pigtown and Basin Lane

THE DAILY walk to and from school in Basin Lane Convent was like a magic tour, with one exception, 'The Spike' or the Workhouse, which was known as the South Dublin Union. The Ma told me the route to take and named off all the places on her finger-tips, using all her fingers, to end at Pigtown and Basin Lane. The route went down Old Kilmainham and passed Lady Lane, Kerin's Place, Watery Lane, Dunlops, Mount Brown, McCaffrey's estate, the Union wall, down Pigtown and into Basin Lane.

'Sure, you can't go wrong. It's all in a straight line till you reach Pigtown...'.

The names fascinated me, as Watery Lane was called Brookfield Road and sometimes I came home by the 40 steps, Bow Lane, the High Road, Rowserstown and Old Kilmainham. Pigtown consisted of whitewashed cottages. In summer the women sat outside their cottages on wooden butter boxes. The convent school stood at the end of Basin Lane, just below the iron footbridge across the Grand Canal, but I don't think I ever used this route.

'Keep away from the Canal' was Ma's war-cry. 'Keep to the tram-tracks and you won't get lost'.

I loved the convent school. Sister Monica remained my favourite and I was also very fond of my two women teachers, Miss Gallagher and Miss Dowling. It was a great school at that time for giving out presents and prizes. Every child in the convent school got a Christmas box. I remember a hurley and ball, and another time a Christmas stocking which I thought was the nicest present in the whole world. There was never a shortage of framed holy pictures and these were all examined by the women in Pigtown: 'Oh, it's lovely. I'd love wan of them for over me bed. Will ya see if Sister Monica could spare me wan of them?'.

'How much did she charge yeh?'. 'Nutin' Missus, nutin'. I got it for nutin'.

'Oh, you must have been a very good boy to get that lovely picture of Saint Ta-rais-a. What does that say?' the woman asked, pointing to the writing on the picture. 'I can't read it without me glasses'.

'Don't mind her,' another woman roared. 'She never wore glasses in her life. Go wan, tell the child ya can't read'.

'Go and clean your dirty windows,' the other woman roared back.

I was getting scared, now, standing between the two women roaring at one another, and I'd have run for me life only the woman was still holding me picture of Saint Ta-Rais-a. So I quickly butted in and said: 'It says, Missus, After my death I will let fall a shower of roses'.

The two women stopped roaring to listen to me and I repeated what it said on the picture.

'A shower of rosies, Maggie,' one woman said to the other. 'Isn't it a beautiful thing Maggie, a shower of roses?'.

'Yis, Hannah,' the other woman answered. 'I'll have to agree with ya, it's a beautiful thing'.

She handed me back the picture and gave me her blessing, pulled the black shawl up over her head and set off towards the convent to see if Sister Monica had another picture of Saint Ta-rais-a for over her bed. The other woman pulled her shawl over her head and followed her neighbour up Basin Lane. I don't know whether they went to the convent or not, but if they did, I'm sure they had Saint Ta-rais-a with them as they went asleep that night.

The convent had a great game called 'cut-the-book'. The teacher held the story book closed between her hands. As it came to my turn to cut the book I was asked which side of the book did I choose, back or front. When the side was chosen I pointed to the place where I wanted the book opened. When the book was opened the first letter of the first word was my letter.

Nearly always I cut the book at the letter A or B and, of course, the game was played on the alphabet. So if no one else got an A or a B I was the winner. On this game I won the most beautiful Easter egg that I ever got in my life. How it wasn't eaten in Pigtown I'll never know, as every man, woman and child came out to admire it. Well, I got it home. The aunt was upstairs, making the beds, and in my rush up the stairs to show her the most beautiful Easter egg in the whole world, didn't I slip on the stairs and me Easter egg was in dust and bits. The aunt could not console me. She insisted that she could tell from the bits, the yellow ribbon and the little blue cotton birds that it must have been a beauty. So we spent all afternoon trying to put the bits together so that me Ma could see the lovely Easter egg when she came home from work. But, like Humpty-Dumpty, we could not put it together again. I was nearly going to go back down to Pigtown to get one of the women to come up and tell Ma how nice the Easter egg was, but Ma said that I would have to break it to eat it and she made a beautiful expression on her face when she tasted a bit and said she'd never eaten anything like it in her life and would I give her the ribbon and birds for her dressing table? So, after all, my day was made but I'd have to tell the women in Pigtown the way it broke into dust.

'Missus, missus, di ya remember me Easter egg, missus?' and I told the story at every cottage. I got loads of sympathy and a cut of bread and jam from my friends in Pigtown and Basin Lane.

The day Alfie Byrne, the Lord Mayor of Dublin, came to the school to open the Basin Walk, he gave every child a big box of Tara Chocolates with a photograph of the Mansion House on the lid, and he let me hold his chain. It was the most important present I ever got, far and above the Easter

egg, and the thrill of holding the chain that he wore around his neck... I went home that day telling everyone I met that the Lord Mayor of Dublin had given me the box of chocolates. I even forgot that everyone else got a box of chocolates. There were two layers of chocolates and this time they couldn't break into dust. So I opened the box in Pigtown.

'Ah, no, son. Take them home to your Mammy'. But I insisted on sharing the Lord Mayor's gift.

Only two or three women took a sweet and burst into praise for Alfie Byrne. 'A terrible decent man, very kind to the childer, and him the Lord Mayor with plenty of other work to be doing. Ah, terrible decent. Must have cost him a fortune for all them 'jockalets'. Lovely jockalets...'.

I loved Alfie Byrne and I was always hoping that the nuns would have something else to open and maybe Alfie would come back with another box of chocolates and maybe the next time he'd let me wear the chain just for a minute.

Although I was afraid of the appearance of the South Dublin Union I used stand and stare at the big brown gate, the high grey-black walls and the iron-barred windows. The gate never seemed to open, but beside the big gate was a small side gate, and out of this gate came old men and women, queer looking people, the women with long grey hair over their shawls, and the men with rough brown suits and shirts with no collars or ties. They never smiled or spoke but looked at me in a frightened sort of a way as they hurried down towards Pigtown.

One morning as I passed the Union gate and turned into Pigtown one woman asked me 'Did you pass the Union gate by yourself?'.

'I did,' I replied.

'Well, yeh will want to watch out' said she, 'that they don't pull you in and give you the Blue Pill'.

The children in school had the same story and a story about a dead nun that comes through the Union wall at twelve midnight.

'Janey, I'm glad I live at the back of the Pipes. I wouldn't like to be you, passing the Union gate. You'd want to watch out or they'll pull you in and give you the Blue Pill and you'll kick the bucket for sure'.

The story of the dead nun, the Blue Pill, the Spike, the Workhouse: I was now terrified of the Union so, every day, I ran like the hammers of hell past the Union gate. One day I heard the gate groan as if to open. I got such a fright that I dropped my schoolbag and I did not wait to pick it up.

A man on a bicycle picked it up and came flying down Mount Brown Hill after me.

'My goodness, the devil must be chasing you,' he said.

'No, mister,' said I, 'it's the Blue Pill and the dead nun'.

The man laughed, got up on his bicycle and rode away.

Another morning as I was getting into my gallop to pass the Union gate I had to stop suddenly to allow a horse and car come out of the gateway. It was a funny looking car, a black square box. Later I was to learn that it was the charity hearse. When the horse and car pulled out, I peeped into the Union. There was a big clock hanging on the wall with a brass frying pan, I thought, swinging back and forth. To the right of the clock was an office with a glass partition and looking out through the glass partition was a nice friendly looking man with silver hair.

He smiled at me and I smiled back.

'Come in,' says he. 'Are ye going to school? Would you like a nice piece of blotting paper?'.

I was half afraid but his smile and the offer of a sheet of blotter made me move in to the office door. Out of a big white pad he pulled a sheet of snow white blotting paper. He handed it to me and it felt warm, soft and nice. When I got to school all the other kids were jealous.

'Where did ya get the sheet of blotter? It's lovely. Give us a bit. Where did ya get it?'

When I told them I got it at the Union gate their faces changed.

'Oh, I wouldn't like to take that. You want to watch that. Don't put it near your mouth. Janey, I don't think I want any'.

But by the end of school their fears quickly vanished away

and when I got to the Union gate there were about 10 or 12 kids there before me, all shouting together: 'Mister, mister, any blotting paper, mister?'.

Whenever the gate was opened it was always the same cry: 'Mister, any blotting paper, mister?'.

The poor gatekeeper must have been driven insane for his kind act in giving me a sheet of blotter. The South Dublin Union must have had a good stock of blotting paper because I never remember a child refused a piece of blotting paper out of the big white pad. It was like a parade of white flags as the children waved their blotting paper going down Mount Brown or the 40 Steps.

The back of the convent school faced the City Basin which, at that time, was like a long swimming pool with its green coloured waters. During the month of May the school May processions were held on the pathways all around the Basin. It was beside the banks of the Basin that our First Holy Communion picture was taken with the late Father O'Callaghan, C.C., James's Street.

The morning of our First Communion in St. James's Church we were given a party by Sister Monica: sweet cakes, sugarstick, peggy's leg and lemonade, and a framed holy picture to mark the occasion. The thing that stands out most in my mind was the practice of our first confession which was held in the nuns' chapel.

We were all scared stiff, not knowing, of course, what was going to happen.

'It was only a trial run, anyway,' me friend said, so it didn't really matter what one said. It was not the real thing. So in I went and told all my sins and all about the Blue Pill and the dead nun.

7

Schooldays in Richmond Barracks

I'M A BIG boy now. I am going to the 'Brothers' school in Keogh Square. I remember the day well, my aunt was all of a fuss. My mother had just left for work and the aunt was getting me organised.

'You have your bag, your pens and pencils, a rubber and a ruler, oh, and your lunch. Did you bless yourself? You did! You're a good boy. But just in case,' she said, 'here's another drop' — she dipped her fingers into the holy water font and gave me another sprinkle of Holy Water, to protect me, and to make sure I'd be alright like, as she said herself, 'well, you're ready now for school at Richmond Barracks'. 'No,' I replied, 'it's St. Michael's, Keogh Square'. 'Well, to me,' says she, 'it will always be Richmond Barracks, they should have pulled it down and built a new school'.

'No, I won't go up with you. Richmond Barracks has too many memories of Easter Week for me.' She opened the hall door, 'there's Paddy Brennan,' said she, follow him up to your school in Richmond Barracks'. I didn't have to follow Paddy Brennan, the whole neighbourhood was going up to school, dozens and dozens of boys and girls. Some had schoolbags on their backs or under their arms, many of the girls had attache cases and others had their books tied with leather straps.

I followed the crowd and noticed at the end of Finnerty's Lane that the boys turned to the right and parted with the

46

girls who walked straight on for Goldenbridge Convent. Within a few moments I was at the school gate. The head Brother told me that I was in Mr. Downer's class, 'first standard,' he said, and that my classroom was the second door in the corridor of the lower building. I had no trouble finding the room as Mr. Downer was waiting with a smile and a handshake. He was a tall young man with black wavy hair and a real happy smile, which made me feel warm and nice.

There and then I adopted him as my father. He didn't know this, of course, but I really loved him and I tried hard to be the best in the class just to please him. The first two years were spent with Mr. Downer and it was during that time that I made my first public speech. Mr. Downer was teaching us Thomas Davis' poem *My Land*. He had a wooden box up beside the blackboard and he was getting the children to stand on the box and recite the poem which was written on the blackboard. The first ten children up on the box didn't come up to Mr. Downer's standard, and he was sort of losing his temper. He roared a few times. I never saw him so angry before. He got up on the box himself and again explained the way he wanted the poem recited. 'Now,' he said, 'is there anyone in the class that can say it like that?' Well, as I said, I loved Mr. Downer, I'd have done anything for him. I'd even have stood on my head on the box to please him, so up went my hand. 'Me Sir,' I said, 'try me Sir.' 'Up you go,' he said. 'Oh! His face looked very cross, so I'd better not fail,' I said to myself. As I was about to step on the box I remembered the way my mother sang or spoke when she was teaching me *The Tri-coloured Ribbon O* and in the same style I recited the poem, folding my arms across my chest as I reached the lines *This native land of mine'*.

When I finished I was afraid to look at Mr. Downer, in case I hadn't said it right. He lifted me off the box... 'Where did you learn to recite like that?' he asked. His face lit up and before I could answer, he stuck his hand in his pocket, took out two pennies and placed them in my hand. That was a fortune in those days, tuppence for a poem, and a poem about Ireland. Oh, how pleased my mother would be to-

MY LAND

She is a rich and rare land,
Oh! she's a fresh and fair land,
She is a dear and rare land—
This native land of mine!

No men than her's are braver,
Her women's hearts ne'er waver;
I'd freely die to save her,
And think my lot divine.

She's not a dull nor cold land,
No, she's a warm and bold land;
Oh! she's a true and old land,
This native land of mine!

Could beauty ever guard her,
And virtue still reward her,
No foe would cross her border,
No friend within it pine!

Oh! she's a fresh and fair land;
Oh! she's a true and rare land;
Yes, she's a rare and fair land—
This native land of mine!

Thomas Davis

night I thought, and for some unknown reason I began to feel sad and my eyes filled up with tears. Mr. Downer noticed this and when I told him about my mother he said, 'they are tears of joy and sadness mixed together, you will make a great public speaker some day'.

By the time school was over I had the poem off by heart, as I wanted to recite it again for my mother and then give her the tuppence, thinking maybe she'd give me back a penny for myself. That night the tears came into my mother's eyes as I recited the poem — she let me keep the tuppence for myself; she wouldn't even take a penny for the poor man, but she did say that I must never again take money for reciting one of Ireland's poems. In future I must recite it for love.

From that day onwards, I got into the habit of reciting poems or singing songs to myself going to and coming from school. Now and again if I was sure no one could hear me, I'd say them out loud. All good things must come to an end, and soon I was to leave Mr. Downer and take my place in Mr. Tunney's class, third standard.

'Tuno' as we called him was a very religious man and he had great devotion to St. Anne. It was my job every Tuesday to take St. Anne's picture out of the press, dust it and display it on the altar. I didn't pray to St. Anne myself, except of a Tuesday, but I used to feel sort of sorry for her, only getting out of the press once a week. Before class ended each Tuesday 'Tuno' gave me the nod to put the picture back in the press. I remarked on this to my mother; she laughed and said, 'Don't worry child, sure some poor women never get out, and Anne is lucky she gets out once a week'. My aunt was listening and she remarked: 'if you could put an air to that, you could sing it'.

I remember 'Tuno' was nearly in tears when we were all leaving for fourth standard. Now he would have to get someone else to look after St. Anne and no one would be able to do such a good job on the May altar as we did, the blue and white paper, the flowers, the polished vases, candles and the beautiful Blessed Virgin Mary made out of the silver paper

50

that came from the bottom of a tea chest. He also wondered if the new children would be able to bring in the same lovely flowers. We reminded him that the purple lilac grew wild and if he was ever short of flowers he could send over a message to fourth standard. 'Tuno' gave us a party: sweets and cakes, 'and be careful with the crumbs'. After school that day the questions and comments came — 'who did ya get? Yis are steeped in luck. Pete's a cinch, he never slaps, he's as soft as putty. Yis are blessed, Pete's a cinch'.

Then came the sale of secondhand books. *Seadna* for fourpence, 'it will cost you wan and a tanner bran' new'; *Carthy's History*, ninepence, 'it's three bob in the shops'. The buying and selling went on for hours and everyone got a bargain. One of the best parts of changing classes was selling your old books and buying secondhand ones for the new class. Books didn't change much in those days and it was always a safe buy to get *Blackcock's Feather, The Lights of Leaca Bawn, Seadna, Muir, Ruir agas Catair,* and *Carthy's History*.

Well, they were right. Pete was a cinch. He was too nice to be a schoolmaster. He never slapped. He never raised his voice, 'easy and slow' he'd say, 'take it easy and slow, the knowledge must come from love'. We were ruined and spoiled by the end of the term. We all agreed that our hands had got too soft and we regretted that Pete hadn't given us even a few biffs to keep our hands in training. Religious and all as 'Tuno' was, he made fair use of the cane, but Pete was a cinch, and our hands were like jelly!

'It's okay if yis are picked for 'Noono's' class, but if yis get 'The Killer', well, may the Lord have mercy on yis — 'Noono's' okay; Brother Noonan, he is in charge of the football team and if you make the team you won't have to do your 'ecker'. He doesn't even give out if he catches you cogging. But now 'The Killer', Brother Keegan, well that's a different kettle of fish — you'd hear 'The Killer' roaring in the Park and he slaps like hell...'

Pete didn't seem too worried as he was drawing the names for the new classes. 'Two lovely Brothers' he said, 'you are all very lucky boys'. My pal's name was drawn from Pete's hat: Brother Noonan. And then came my name — Brother Keegan, 'The Killer', I nearly fainted.

The bell rang. Pete wished us all good luck and if we ever needed his advice we were always welcome. As I was going down to the school gate who did I meet but 'The Killer' himself. I declare to God he was seven foot tall, a big giant of a man. His fist was nearly as big as my head and I was only two feet over a jam-jar in height. I tried to force a smile as he came nearer. He stopped, glared at me and roared, 'What have you got to smile about? Are you coming into my class? You are, well, well, well, I'll be looking forward to meeting you, now go on home and smile at that'. Oh, its true I tell you, I was nearly going to go on the Gur that night, but instead I banged my hands fifty times on Mellon's wall at the second lock on the Grand Canal. I gave my hands another few bangs on Finnerty's wall on the way to school the next morning.

'The Killer' was sitting at his desk as I opened the door. He looked at me and smiled, then he looked at the clock, two minutes to nine. 'You made it,' he said, 'and you don't seem to be smiling today'. I tried to force another smile but it wouldn't come. Maybe I should have went on the Gur after all. 'The Killer' pointed out my place, so I sat down and put my bag under the desk. The room was silent except for the ticking of the clock and then it struck nine. As soon as the ninth chime sounded 'The Killer' was on his feet for the morning prayers. As the prayers ended he addressed the class. 'Do you know what they call me in this school?' he asked. 'No Sir, no Sir,' a chorus of voices answered. 'Come now,' he said, 'surely your brothers have told you.' 'No Sir, no Sir,' everyone answered. 'You,' he said, pointing at me. 'You tell them what they call me. Stand up there and tell them all the stories you have heard and the name they call me.' The way in which he asked the questions told me that I wasn't going to get tuppence for the right answer. I stood up quickly and shouted, 'They call you 'The Killer' Sir, they say you're 'The Killer'.' He stood up, threw his arms up in the air and gave a loud laugh. He now really looked like a giant. He lowered his arms and raised his black cincture up under his armpits, he walked up and down the room laughing and saying: 'So I'm 'The Killer' now. I used to be 'The Bulldog'.'

The cincture was waving like a black flag, and as it began to slide down his chest he kept pulling it back up under his armpits. Most Brothers wore this cincture around their waists, but 'The Killer' wore his up under his armpits.

I was later to learn that the cincture never got in his way when he used the leather strap. Some Brothers allowed the cincture to get mixed up with the cane stick or leather, but 'The Killer' had slapping down to a fine art. The leather always fell across the four fingers where it hurt most. 'The Killer' told me to sit down, and said I was a very honest and truthful boy.

The first week passed by: it was spent getting to know one another, the lessons he had in mind and the results he expected. As the days flashed by I came to love 'The Killer'. He was really as gentle as a lamb, his bark was worse than his bite. He seldom slapped; in fact, the leather was only used when we were bold, or caught talking or reading penny horribles when we should have been reading our religious handbook. I learned a lot from 'The Killer'. He was very fair, no pets or favourites, and he was a dedicated teacher who could show human kindness in the strangest ways.

He made us all take the pledge that we wouldn't mitch during his term, and I don't think anyone ever broke that pledge. I didn't. In fact, after the pledge I wasn't interested in mitching. 'The Killer' always had a new idea every day, it was he who told us 'to save for the rainy day'. But we thought that was mad, sure if it was raining you wouldn't be able to go out and spend your few bob! It should have been 'save for the sunny day'.

He got us all to save Fry's Cocoa coupons, and when we had a certain number collected, he told us we could get a Mickey Mouse watch which we could raffle among the class, or a large box of assorted chocolates and we would all get a few each. We didn't get many chocolates in those days and we didn't fancy our chances of winning the Mickey Mouse watch, so we all voted for the big box of chocolates. I'll never forget the day the box of chocolates arrived. 'The Killer' was like Santa Claus going around all the desks counting out the lovely sweets. After the divide, he told us there were still four sweets left in the box and when we suggested that he eat them himself he blushed like a child, he went all shy. He couldn't speak for a moment or two. Then he thanked us and said he would always remember this day. He used the empty box for his pens and notebooks and it always stood in the centre of his desk. Now and again we caught him rubbing his hand along the thatch roof of the white cottage that was pictured on the empty chocolate box.

I felt sad the day we left him. He said he hated goodbyes and then roared, 'Goodbye, be good. Don't forget the 'Old Killer' in your prayers'. He stormed out the door. It was summer holiday time. No one asked us who did ya get. No one seemed to care. It was just a brisk sale of schoolbooks, and after the holliers we would be going into 'Macker's' class, sixth standard. No one had much to say about 'Macker' so we would just have to wait and see for ourselves.

There was one Sunday Mass that we all hated. It was the one where the priest said, 'And all the schools of the Parish will re-open tomorrow, Monday. Parents are asked to send their children regularly and punctually to school'....

'Macker' — Mr. McDonald, our new teacher, had a favourite saying — 'Holy house, come downstairs and listen to this' — and whenever we heard that saying addressed to us, we knew we were in for a lousy day. The first month was like hell and we were all very glad that our pledge against mitching ended with 'The Killer's' term. School became a bore. 'The Mitch' or 'The Jer', as others called it, became a joy. Swimming, looking for birds' nests, climbing trees, scutling, playing on the barges on the Liffey. The adventure of hiding our schoolbags, and the art of learning to write 'excuse letters' with a scrawl of a signature so that 'Macker' would think that our mothers had written the letter.

That was the term when I became a real rebel, a little

54

jester, always looking for a funny situation and up to every devilment. That was the term I was bashed by 'Macker', my mother and the head Brother. My aunt also took a hand at it, now and again.

I organised an ink-drinking competition and nearly poisoned half the class: on the line — twelve biffs.

Laughed during prayers: on the line — twelve biffs.

Put mud in hungry Horace's lunch-box, which he ate: on the line — six biffs.

Caught getting the cog: on the line — six biffs.

Caught reading the *Beano* comic: on the line — twelve biffs.

About this time the head Brother kept a black diary and if one's name got into it one had to parade in front of the whole school in the big gym and, of course, take one's medicine: six biffs, three on each hand. Once a month the whole school assembled in the big gym. The head Brother produced his diary and my name was always among the first ten. In later years I learned that in this same big gym, in Richmond Barracks in 1916, other men, G-men of Dublin Castle, appeared with little black diaries and read out the names of men who were sent forward to Kilmainham Jail for execution and a quick-lime grave in Arbour Hill.

During all my years in the school we were never told anything of the school building's connection with the Easter Week Rising. History lessons ended with Parnell, 'the uncrowned King of Ireland'. We sat for the Primary Certificate and when the results arrived the entire class had passed except me.

'Holy house, come downstairs and listen to this'. I was really the black sheep now, but the rebel in me was strong and I didn't give a damn. 'Shag the Primary. I'll show them'. I was allowed go forward to seventh standard on condition that I would return to have another bash at the Primary Cert.

This was to be my last year in school at Richmond Barracks. 'Roney Boy' or Mr. Rowan, as we called him, was a gentleman, but, like Pete, he was too nice to be a schoolmaster. I enjoyed my year with him. In fact, I never mitched.

He taught us how to respect things, but he wasn't very fussy when he was checking exercise books. He never looked at the books, but just walked up and down beside the desks, putting his mark with a red coloured marker on each exercise book. It did not take us long to spot this, so in due course, he was marking all sorts of things in the exercise books.

For the bet of a big steel marble I chanced putting a copy of *The Beano* on my desk. As he came near me, my knees were knocking together and I was breaking out in a cold sweat. But I was dying to own the big steel marble, so down went his coloured marker and *The Beano* was signed unnoticed.

I'd hate to think what would have happened if he had looked down at the desk. I sat again for the Primary Cert. and after six hours, forty-eight twisted ears, twenty-four twisted hair locks, three belts on the back of the neck and all the right answers whispered in my ear, I passed the Primary Cert.

'Shag the Primary! I'll show yiz!'

I left school that term as my widowed mother could not afford the fee or the price of the books to allow me to continue at James's Street Secondary School. That was the first time in my life that I was very thankful to God that we hadn't any money.

I made a vow at the age of thirteen years that I would never sit in a classroom or attend another school for the rest of my life. I had only one ambition now, to get a job to pay the rent for Ma, and to do that job to the very best of my ability.

8

The Magical Brickfields

THE FIRST TIME we discovered the Brickfields it was almost too good to be true. We all agreed that it was a magical place, real cowboy and Indian country, with wild goats and piebald ponies, a rocky mountain, a mill race with stepping stones, tunnels to explore, and iron wagons on iron tracks on which we played trams and miners. It even had a tip-head where yellow vans dumped millions of rotten bananas and Wills' vans dumped broken and torn cigarettes. For every four rotten bananas there was always at least one good one, sometimes two, on each stalk, so we were never short of a feed of bananas or a smoke.

The Rooney pickers didn't bother with things like those as they were of no value and we had these dumps all to ourselves. The Rooneys went after lead, copper wire, brass, coal cinders, books, magazines, prams, buckets, porter bottles and jam jars. They didn't seem to mind the grey-white seagulls spitting on them but we used chase the seagulls away: 'Go 'way. Shag off, seagulls. These are our bananas'. The seagulls always got the message and left us to pick the good fruit out of the black rotten mountain of bananas. When the meal was over we poked around the cigarette dump and got plenty of free *Gold Flake* and *Three Castles* cigarettes. Then we moved around watching the Rooney pickers, their expert hands and eyes working all over the tiphead. They worked in pairs and now and again they would shout across to one another: 'Mary, Mary, four bottles and a jam jar'. 'Thanks Christie, thanks. Tell Kate I've got cinders and a lump of lead'. On and on they'd work, the silence broken only when one had found something for the other.

Across the millrace and between the rocky mountain and the shell of the old brickmill building stood two favourite spots. The first was the men's pitch-and-toss school: no children allowed, so we had to climb the rocky mountain to look down on the wide circle and see the boxman keeping the circle wide with his big leather belt. 'Clear the box, clear the box,' he'd roar as he lashed out with the buckle end of his leather belt. 'Who's for the flyers? Heads a quid. Heads two, four, six, eight or half-a-note. Heads a dollar. Heads a bob. Heads a bob'. It was better than watching a football match and we had a grandstand seat on top of the rocky mountain. Then one of our gang would shout out 'Heads a bob, heads a bob'. Then, like the seagulls, we had to scatter as the men told us to shag off in no uncertain manner.

The second favourite spot was Martin's hut. Martin was an ex-British soldier who fought in the First World War and who lived all alone with his dog in a little hut-like house which he had built himself out of stones, bricks and mud. It was a very small one-room hut, with a stretched-type bed on the floor. He had a good open fire and chimney, a small card table, one chair and two biscuit tins filled with clay each side of the fire. These made two more comfortable seats. Martin lived on a small pension and his pickings on the tip-head. All the fuel for his fire came from the same place. It was neat and tidy with a clay floor. He drew his washing water from the mill-race and his drinking water from the hot arch spring which ran alongside of the rocky mountain. Martin himself was a very neat, clean man. He shaved with an open razor every day. He was the sort of a man it would be hard to put an age on. He looked 50 or 60 but he could have been in his early 40's. He didn't speak much but just sat at the fire, smoking his pipe, thinking, thinking and thinking. He had a lovely silver pocket-watch and he always made sure that we left his

hut early.

'Time to go, now, boys. Thanks for the visit. You're welcome anytime. No, I'm never lonely. I always have the dog and my pipe and a place to lay my head', he'd say. Then he'd laugh and show the two gold fillings in his clear white teeth. He had a small moustache and now and again he would wax the ends 'just for a change,' as he'd say himself. He wore a short-sleeved, open-necked khaki shirt in summer and winter. His skin was the colour of bronze. His hair was grey, close-cut, 'British army style,' he told us, 'and easy to keep clean'. He kept only the bare essentials in food: 'Too many rats around,' he said. Then he'd address the dog: 'Rats, Jack, rats'. The dog would jump up and sniff around the hut, along by the bed, look at his master, bark a few times and then lie down again. 'Yeh can't fool Jack,' he'd say. 'Jack's the boy for the rats'.

Martin would give us a cup of tea but nothing to eat: 'I've only a bit of bread left and that's for me breakfast'. As soon as the tea was over, out came the silver watch. 'Time to go, boys'. The flames from the fire would light up the hut but we noticed that Martin used silver-rimmed glasses and a halfpenny candle when reading the evening newspaper. I don't remember seeing any books in the hut, only a few newspapers which always seemed to be several months old. Martin didn't mind reading January's newspapers in June or July.

We knew that the tinkers (or gypsies, as we called them) owned the piebald ponies, but who owned the bloody goats? 'Them's wild, I tell ya, them's wild,' someone would roar and then came the answer: 'Wild, me eye. Whoever heard of a wild goat with a bloody bell around his neck?'. Wild or not, bell or no bell, many's the mouthful of milk I got from the goats in the Brickfields. I think they liked being milked. They always stood still. But then, I suppose the poor old goat had no option with 12 boys holding him down. The piebald ponies were hard to catch but now and again we got the occasional bareback ride, holding on to the mane for dear life and sliding off as soon as he stopped at a heap of bricks.

The Brickfields were laid out like potato drills. The bricks were about five feet high, running in long lines like small mountains. Each line of bricks had its own tunnel opening, wagons and tracks. In the centre of the Brickfield was a large quarry, like a large round lake. No one swam in it. Some said it had no bottom. It was a fisherman's paradise and was loaded with perch, roach eel and, some said, a few salmon. But I saw more dead new-born babies fished out of it than I ever saw salmon. The two local expert fishermen were the late Mr. Mason and Mr. Kearney. It was a treat to watch these men casting their lines. They would stand well away from each other. They didn't like spectators and would be annoyed if one spoke in case the fish would be scared away. This did not go down too well with us talkative children: 'How many did you catch, Mr. Kearney?'. We never got an answer and, if we kept asking we were told to clear off. Old Mr. Mason never answered either.

We started a new game: 'Mr. Kearney, did ya know that Mr. Mason caught six?'. Then we'd run around the quarry to Mr. Mason and say: 'Mr. Mason, Mr. Mason, Mr. Kearney's after catching seven'. When we got fed up at this we ended up by throwing a big house brick into the quarry in the hope that we would get a good chase across the Brickfields. But that didn't work either. Both men just took out their pipes, lit up, sat back and had a smoke.

The front entrance to the Brickfields was at the First Lock on the Grand Canal, where Davitt Road starts today. The rocky mountain stood where the park is today. The rear end of the Brickfields was at the railings of Iveagh ground. At that time St. James's Gate Football Team was in the F.A.I. League. O'Reilly was their captain and Webster, their goalkeeper. The rear entrance was our private entrance to all the Gate's football matches. We never missed a Saturday match and no one was collecting admission fees, and we climbed over the high spiked iron railings and bunked in. All went well until a steward spotted us and, from that day onwards, the stewards always patrolled the rear entrance.

'Mister, mister: let's in and we'll cheer for ya. Will ya, mister? We'll cheer for ya, won't we?'. 'Yes, mister,' a chorus of voices would ring out. 'Let's in and we'll cheer for ya'. 'Get to bloody hell out of here,' the stewards shouted through the railings. Suddenly our tune would change: 'Shag the Gate. Shag the Gate. We hope today they'll be bate. The Gate, the Gate, we hope they're late for the goals. Mister, let's in and we'll cheer for ya. Will ya, mister, we'll cheer for ya?'. And then again: 'Shag the Gate. Shag the Gate'.

One steward made the sorry mistake of throwing a stone at us. 'Was he mad?' we asked and we sitting in the Brickfields with only millions and millions of bricks and stones. That was the rock that the steward perished on. The stewards soon scattered as a hail of bricks landed on them. A few moments later we scattered when two big red-necked policemen appeared on the scene. That ended our free private entrance to Iveagh Grounds via the Brickfields. But even with that great loss the Brickfields were still magical and, while on our way to milk a goat, explore a tunnel or ride a piebald pony, we came up with an idea to beat the stewards in Iveagh Grounds and give our team, 'The Gate', our fullest support.

All Guinness's workers had a little red membership card which admitted free an adult or two children to the football matches in Iveagh Grounds. Two children from Suir Road went on this pass every Saturday. They merely had to show the pass and were allowed enter the Ground by the members' gate on the Crumlin Road. We arranged with them to pass the pass out through the iron railings at the paying turnstile entrance. I'm not joking. That pass went in and out of Iveagh Grounds railings like Darkie Bluebells. Often we got as many as thirty children in on the same pass. The stewards were very diligent and brainy in those days and, when the next season came around the stewards checked the numbers on each pass and, of course, I was caught. The pass was confiscated. The Gardai were sent for. That was bad enough, until one of the stewards remembered the cry: 'Shag the Gate, shag the Gate'. 'You're wan of them,' he said. 'No, mister, no. Up the Gate. Up the Gate. Give it to Reilly. Great save, Webster. Come on, the Gate. In around the house. On your

bike, Reilly. On your bike'. It's true we were supporters
but he didn't believe me, not even when I named the whole
team for him. They let me go. The next time I'd go to jail
and, if they ever found me in the Ground without a ticket,
they would kill me.

On my way home that day as I crossed the magical Brickfields I got another good idea. From now on, shag the Gate,
I'd support Dolphin and, besides, they were not too fussy if
you bunked in over the wall.

The day we found Martin's hut pulled down we knew
something was going to happen. Within days the builders
moved in. The rocky mountain was removed by explosives.
The quarry was filled in. The bricks and stones were carted
away. The old mill was in dust. The tinkers moved out
like a large wagon train as the colourful caravans, piebald
ponies and wild goats headed for the Naas Road.

The tip-head was closed. Gone, too, were the seagulls and
the Rooney pickers. All sorts of rumours were floating
around. A new football pitch. A factory. A soldiers' barracks.
A hospital. Another church. As the months passed by, the
new housing scheme of north Crumlin was taking shape:
Mourne, Galtymore, Sperrin, Cooley, Slievebloom, Keeper,
Benbulbin... beautiful names for the magical Brickfields of
my childhood days.

9

A Volcano at the Hellfire Club

SIKEY O'TOOLE WAS our local philosopher. He was more than that. He was a genius as well. There was nothing in the world that Sikey didn't know. You name it and Sikey knew the answer. He should have been a school teacher instead of collecting empty porter bottles for 'The Welcome Inn'. Many people said that Sikey was a professor in a college but that he took to drink and that the college had sacked him. Another thing about Sikey, despite all his knowledge and his brains: he had a perpetual smile and laugh and was always in good humour. Sikey wasn't a bit like our schoolmaster who, when answering questions had a face like Dracula the monster and gave the impression that all his knowledge was weighing heavy on his mind and hurting him. No, Sikey always had a nice happy smile that lit up his face and made his eyes twinkle. Sikey had a baldy head which, he claimed, was the proof of his brains or, as he would say himself: 'Grass can't grow on a busy street'.

Sikey always reminded me of the happy face that used to be seen on one side of the old *Mac's Smile* razor blade. We learned more from Sikey after school than we did in the classrooms. All about the moon, the sun, the stars; what kept the canal barges up in the canal locks; why they didn't sink and all about the Banshee and the old Green Lady who walked at midnight on the canal waters.

Sikey was a gifted storyteller and often I wondered how

64

long it took him to collect all the empty porter bottles, because he seemed to spend all his time telling stories or answering questions on the canal banks or at the corner passage at Kickham Road. It was Sikey who told us about the money on the E.S.B. poles.

'Do you see them little white pots up there on top of the E.S.B. pole?' he asked. 'Well, there's a half-a-crown in each one of them. There has to be,' he said. 'It's there to help conduct the electricity along the wires. Yes, boys, a half-a-crown in every little pot'. Before Sikey was out of sight we were all counting the little white pots..: 'Two, four, six. Janey, sixteen pots on every pole. Two bleedin' quid on every pole. Will ya look at all the poles, thousands of them!'. Soon our slings were out as a mad search was made of the canal bank for suitably sized stones. Crack, crack, crack – for every ten shots with the slings a few little white pots would disappear into smithereens. Then Murphy's voice rang out: 'Okay, okay, hold it. That's enough. Stop firin'. We hit four. That's ten bob. They must have fell on the bank – the half-dollars, I mean'. The slings were put away as we searched for the silver half-crowns. In our minds' eyes we saw the horse and harp on the half-crown pieces. But that's the only place we saw them, for there wasn't sign nor light of them on the canal banks. 'Maybe they fell into the water,' said Murphy, as he went to the edge of the bank and gazed into the green depths of the Grand Canal. The water was shallow and one could see the bed. But there was no sign of the half-crowns. 'Let's try another few pots,' said someone else. 'Let's go in, for a swim,' said Murphy. 'Let's go home for our tea,' said Bonker, 'I think Sikey was getting it up for us'. We looked at Bonker. 'How dare you,' we said. 'If Sikey knows, that's good enough for us. Maybe the half-crowns are nailed to the poles'. 'Do you think we could climb them?' asked Murphy. 'Naw,' said someone else. 'You'd never climb them poles. Sure, there are no grips on them'. 'Look, fellas,' said Murphy, 'here's Sikey again'.

Sure enough, there he was, coming down along the canal bank, his big wicker basket half full of empty porter bottles sitting on one part of his backside and caught with his right arm which made him walk sort of sideways, like a crab. As he reached us a chorus of voices cried out: 'Sikey, Sikey, we didn't find any half-crowns'. Sikey let drop his basket of bottles. We could almost feel the weight of it the way it hit the ground with a thud. Then he looked up at the pole, noticing the missing white pots. He looked around at each one of us and started to look across the canal towards the Brickfields and the Dublin Mountains. Sikey never spoke, but kept gazing across the canal. He wasn't smiling, either. In fact he had a very cross expression on his face. With that, Murphy burst out: 'What is it, Sikey? What's wrong? What are you looking at? Tell us, Sikey, tell us!'. The little white pots and the half-crowns were soon forgotten as we looked from the basket of bottles to Sikey, but still he stood there, gazing, never saying a word. All of a sudden he turned, picked up his basket quickly and, in a strange voice said: 'Yis'd better git home and git to the chapel quick for Confession. Mind yis, git to the chapel quick, for it will surely be crowded to-night. See that,' he said, pointing across to a fire on the mountains, 'that's a volcano and it will sweep across here before nine o'clock tonight. We will all be killed, roasted alive. That volcano will spread. Look at it, it's getting bigger every minute'. We looked again at the fire on the mountains and it did seem to be getting bigger and bigger. Sikey moved off with a bit of a run and shouted back: 'Git home and git to the chapel. We will be all dead tonight'.

No one waited to argue or to doubt Sikey. There was a mad dash down Southern Cross Avenue and no one stopped till we reached our homes in Goldenbridge, Kilmainham. I pushed in the back kitchen door and there was all the family, sitting at the table, having tea. They were laughing and talking as I burst in.

'What are yiz doing?' I asked, 'having tea and laughing, and the volcano only up the road. Why are yiz not in the chapel?'. It was my older brother who spoke first. 'Where did you get your volcano?' he asked. 'That's only a gorse fire on the mountains and it's miles from here. You can see fires like them any day of the week' he added. 'It's not a fire,' I said, 'It's a bloody volcano. Sikey said it was a volcano, and he knows more than you do'. The rest of the family ignored me and went on with their tea and laughter. 'Well, okay,' I said, 'If youse want to die without Confession I don't' and I ran out of the kitchen, up Goldenbridge Avenue, down Connolly Avenue and towards the gate of St. Michael's Chapel. As I got to the gate I was breathless, so I sat down to rest on the chapel doorstep. I felt lonely and afraid and I began to cry for my mother. I wondered if I should go back for my mother. She wouldn't come anyway, so what was the use in going back? Maybe the volcano was down in Goldenbridge Avenue by now. Yes, they could be all dead and there I was on my own. I got up and pushed in the chapel door. The chapel was in semi-darkness and I thought the people must be praying in the dark. After a short while my eyes got used to the darkness and I noticed that the chapel was empty. There were a few candles lighting at St. Joseph's shrine. There was the red lamp in front of the High Altar and the blue lamp at Our Lady's Altar, but where were the people? They must all have gone to the Oblates or to James's Street Church, or maybe to the Little Sisters' Chapel on the Circular Road.

Then I noticed a lone figure kneeling at St. Joseph's shrine. It was the parish priest himself. 'Excuse me, Father,' I said. 'When will you be hearing Confession?'. He looked up as if he had got a fright, or maybe he was worried about the volcano. 'Confession,' he said. 'Wait now. Yes, next Saturday at 11 o'clock'. Next Saturday, I said to myself. Sure we will all be dead before Saturday. Sikey said we'd all be dead tonight, and tonight's Thursday. I wondered if the priest knew about the volcano or was he only saving himself?

'Excuse me, Father, but there's a volcano coming down the road. Do you know that, Father?'. He looked up again and he said with a smile: 'Well, me son, if it comes this way I hope it heats up this church'.

Then he gave a loud laugh, which wasn't fair, because we were never allowed to talk, never mind laugh, in the church. The way he laughed at my volcano told me that Sikey had been getting it up for us again.

I came out of the chapel door and walked slowly down Bulfin Road. In a way I was sorry that there was no volcano to kill us. After all, I was in time for Confession and that's all that mattered. Now I would have to go on living, but I could never trust or believe Sikey again, and life without Sikey was going to be terrible dull and lonely.

10

Me Proddy Dick Friend

HE LIVED A few roads away from our house. I don't really know how we became friends. Maybe it was because I got fed up jeering him and then began to feel sorry for him: he looked to me so funny yet so lonely in his little pill-box hat and white belt. He was a member of the Boys' Brigade and attended regularly at all its meetings.

He always gave me a smile and a wave when passing the corner. Twice he stopped and gave me a few sweets and a copy of 'Film Fun' comic which, he said, he was finished with. In return, I gave him a handful of cigarette pictures. From that day we were true friends. We often played marbles together or spun our wooden tops side by side. He had a lovely top, one with colours, and, as it spun, the top seemed like a blue and white star. Mine was only a plain, yellow one, yet he liked my one better than his own and often used his twine and stick whip on mine long after his coloured one had spun out. I don't think he had the knack of spinning a top, so I gave him a few lessons and showed him the part of the top where the whip should land.

I always beat him at marbles as well, yet the next day he would have a new supply of 'glassers' or white chalk ones. Now and again I let him win a game as I felt mean taking all his marbles. But he didn't seem to mind and said that his dad always brought home pocket-fulls. He wore nice clothes and his pocket watch was no Mickey Mouse one, it was a real watch, with a loud tick and jet-black hands against green numbers and a green dial. He told me you could tell the time in the dark with it, but I thought he was codding me.

'Oh, it's true,' he said. 'It glows in the dark,' and he got down on his knees and put the watch under his jacket coat.

'Look,' he said, 'look, see how the numbers shine'.

I couldn't see any difference, but to please him I said 'Yeh! I see it. I see it'.

'You don't,' he said. 'You're only letting on, the same way as you let me win at marbles. Why do you do that?'.

'Do what? Do what?' I said, getting angry that I couldn't see the watch as he saw it.

'You always want to please me. Why do you do that? Is it because we are friends?'.

'Yes, because we are friends,' I answered, 'and I'm your only friend, or am I?'.

'Well, up here you are,' he said. 'No one else plays with me, but I've lots of friends in the B.B.'.

'What's the B.B.?' I asked.

'The Boys' Brigade,' he said. 'It's like the Scouts. We play games and do drill and jump over horses'.

I was thinking of the piebald horses in the Brickfields and I couldn't imagine Dick jumping over them. He laughed and explained it was a wooden horse and he drew one with a piece of chalk on the footpath.

'Look,' he said, 'the next time we have a B.B. inspection I'll get you a free ticket and you can come and see for yourself'.

Then he added 'It's a pity, you just missed one last month. Are you in the Boy Scouts?', he asked.

'No,' I said. 'I tried to join in Dolphin's Barn but the Scoutmaster put us out for causing trouble. We tied all his ropes in big black knots and he said we were too young, to come back in a few years, as it would take some job to make Scouts out of us. Do you carry the pole or a brush handle?' I asked him.

'No,' he said, 'I don't carry a pole'.

Dick was never allowed out after tea so our playtime

71

ended at six o'clock. I didn't see him every day, and often a week went by and he never seemed to be around. A few times I was going to knock on his door and ask was he coming out to play, but, as I got near his house, I always changed my mind and returned to the corner. Dick was an only child. He seemed to have everything, yet he wasn't spoiled or greedy.

I began to miss him so, after a few weeks, I took up courage to knock on his door. His mother opened it and told me that he was sick and in the Adelaide Hospital, in Peter Street. Dick spent several weeks in hospital and, when he came home, he went to the country for a month's holiday. The next time I saw him he looked different, very pale and thin, but he had got much taller. He was looking down at me, now, and he didn't seem to want to play my games. So we sat on the wall of the garden outside his house. He never spoke a word. After a while he said he was going in and he didn't know when he would see me again. He looked sick and tired and lonely.

'Don't go yet,' I said. 'It's not nearly tea-time. Sure it's not long since we got our dinner. Come on down to our corner and we will play soap bubbles'.

His face lit up and he said, 'okay'. Down we went and he walked slowly while I ran ahead to get my penny white clay pipe out of the shed in the back garden. Within a few moments we were sitting in the middle of the gang at the corner dipping the pipes into a basin of soapy water and blowing bubbles all over the place.

Dick and I were sharing my pipe. Things were going great until one of the other boys pushed Dick as he was dipping in the pipe. Dick went sprawling all over the basin, spilling the contents on the footpath and breaking my white clay pipe.

'Now look what you've done,' the boys shouted as Dick lay in the soapy water, his eyes on the broken pipe. He took a few moments to get up and wipe his clothes. Then he turned to look at the boy who had pushed him.

'Why did you do that?' he asked.

'Because you're a Proddy-Woddy, that's why!'.

The other boys also chanted 'Proddy-Woddy, Proddy-Woddy'. Dick ignored them and told me his dad would buy me a new pipe. As he was about to walk away another chorus of 'Proddy-Woddy' rang out. Dick waited until he had got some distance away and then he roared out:

'Catholic, Catholic go to Mass, riding on the Devil's ass'.

The chase began but Dick was a fast runner, so eventually we all stood outside his house shouting

> *'Proddy, Proddy on the wall*
>
> *Proddy, Proddy, you're going to fall.*
>
> *Hold on, by day and night,*
>
> *And read your Bible by candle light'.*

Back at the corner the gang turned on me — 'It's all your fault. You brought him down. He's your friend, a bloody Proddy-Woddy'.

'What's wrong with that?' I asked.

'Well, it's not right,' they answered, 'and you the prefect of our Guild in the Sacred Heart Sodality. I'm sure if Father Brady knew that, you'd lose the prefect's job'.

'Oh, I wouldn't like to be you, going to Confession,' they said. 'Father, my friend's a Proddy. That's bad enough, but wait till you tell him about going to Mass on the Devil's ass. Oh, you will have to give up the prefect's job'.

Now, I was very fond of the prefect's job and it made me feel very important collecting the pennies on a Saturday morning and paying the money into the vestry. Father Brady said I'd the best and biggest guild in the Sodality and my monthly collection was nearly three shillings. The word 'prefect' sounded very nice. The Proddy or the prefect — this seemed to be the choice that evening at the corner, and to make matters worse, one of the gang had gone into his house and brought out the 'big caddier'. He flicked over the pages until he found what he was looking for.

'There it is,' he said, 'in black and white: 'Outside the Catholic Church there is no redemption'. Do you hear that?' he asked me. 'No redemption. No redemption'. I didn't know the meaning of the word 'redemption' and I didn't want to show me ignorance. So I just said: 'So what? No redemption'.

The words sounded very cold, like the sign in Dowling's shop window: 'No Cigarettes'. If it had said: 'Sorry, no redemption', it might not have been too bad, as if they were sorry about it. But the 'sorry' was missing, just the cold words: 'no redemption' and the choice, the Proddy or the prefect, and the 'Catholic, Catholic go to Mass, riding on the Devil's ass', were all ringing in my ears. So I decided to go home and ask my Aunt Mary the meaning of the word 'redemption'.

As I pushed in the kitchen door Aunt Mary was washing clothes on a large brown washing board which stuck up out of the sink. The kitchen smelled of soap and washing. She didn't see or hear me come in and she was singing and talking to herself as she scrubbed the clothes with a bar of carbolic soap.

'Sing, oh, hurrah, let England quake, the West's awake, the West's awake'. And then, as she pushed the clothes down the board into the water, she said: 'Oh, if I was a man I'd have killed Lloyd George', and then she burst into another song:

> Fill up, once more, we'll drink a toast
> to comrades far away.
> No nation on this earth can boast
> of braver heart than they,
> And though they sleep in dungeon's deep,
> unfree, outlawed and banned,
> We love them yet
> We'll ne'er forget
> The felons of our land'

'Oh! If I was a man, I'd have killed Lloyd George.'

I didn't think this was the best time to ask her the question so I slipped out again unnoticed. An hour later I went in again. This time the aunt was ironing clothes by the light of the range fire. Her shadow flickered on the wall as she lifted the red-hot iron from the bars of the range fire. It was the old-fashioned type of iron and, to test it, to see if it was hot enough, or too hot, she spat on the face of the iron, and the spittle rolled down like little white snowballs.

She let the iron cool a minute and then lifted it up again and banged it down on the blanket.

'Oh,' she said again, 'If I was a man I'd have killed Lloyd George', and then she burst into another song: 'We are the boys of Wexford who fought with heart and hand...'

Then she spotted me but continued the song, in a strong clear voice with plenty of feeling, so that I could nearly see the captain's daughter in man's attire fighting for liberty.

'Well,' she said, 'what do you want? It's not teatime yet. Why are you not out playing?'

I sat there fascinated, half afraid of her and watching her shadow flicker up and down the wall, thinking I was glad my name wasn't Lloyd George.

'Well,' she said again, 'have you no mouth?'

'It's now or never,' I said to myself. Then I burst out: 'What's the meaning of the word 'redemption'?'

'Oh,' said she, 'that's a big word for a little fellow like you. Where did you hear that?'

'It's in the Caddier,' I said, and added the other piece: 'Outside the Catholic Church there is no redemption'.'

'Rubbish, child. Rubbish,' she said. 'In My Father's house there are many mansions'. 'Redemption' means redeemed or saved. But what's there is rubbish, child, rubbish: 'In My Father's house there are many mansions'.'

I began to think that Heaven was like a tenement house and Dick would be in one room or mansion and I'd be in another. I wondered would there be stairs in the house and could I go up to Dick or could he come down to me? It would be terrible to think that there would be no stairs in

76

the house. In that case, I suppose, we could wave out the window to one another. But, it would be better if we could be in the same room. So I went asleep that night with the words 'no redemption, no redemption' and 'rubbish, child, rubbish' and 'in My Father's house there are many mansions', all ringing in my ears.

A few days later I met Dick and I gave him my chestnut, the conqueror of fourteen, I told him. He said he was sorry about the Devil's ass and Mass and that his dad wasn't forgetting to get me the new clay pipe.

'It's okay, Dick,' I said, putting my arm around his shoulder. 'In My Father's house there are many mansions and I don't care if I lose the prefect's job.'

He looked at me as if I was mad, but I was wondering if I should give him my big steel marble as well, just in case there were no stairs in the house.

The next day he had the new pipe. It was a real fancy one and cost more than a penny. Dick showed me his school books, all marked 'High School, Dublin', and one of the books was 'The Life of Robert Emmet'.

I was surprised at this, as we had a picture of Robert Emmet, but Dick told me he was a Proddy, too. I didn't want to argue with him. But that was another question for me Aunt Mary. Robert Emmet a Proddy? No, he couldn't be.

The Aunt Mary was polishing the range with 'Zebra Black Lead'.

'Well, what's it, this time?' she asked.

'Robert Emmet,' I said, 'Was he a Proddy?'

'He was the finest Irishman we ever had,' she said and then started singing:

Bold Robert Emmet, the darlin' of Ireland,
Bold Robert Emmet, he died with a smile,
Saying, farewell companions, most loyal and daring.
I gave up me life for the Emerald Isle'.

'Oh, if I was a man, I'd have killed Lloyd George.'

So I decided that Dick would be with Robert Emmet when he died. I asked Dick if he knew Lloyd George but he said he didn't and asked me why.

'Oh,' I said, 'me Aunt Mary wants to kill him'.

11

The Devil in Inchicore

'WELL, THEN, it's fixed,' he said. 'Thursday next, 3.30 p.m., after school'. 'Yeh, Okay, It's fixed,' I answered as I stood still at the Passage Gate, my schoolbag under my arm, my left hand fiddling with the chrome buckle and strap which opened and closed the brown leather bag.

'You won't let me down?' he asked, looking at me in a hard sort of a way, weighing me up in his mind. 'No,' he said again. 'I don't think you will. Let me down, I mean'.

A few seconds later he was gone. My mouth was dry. My knees were almost knocking together like a pair of bone rattlers. A few times I put my free hand on my hair to make sure that it wasn't standing up straight. I began to wonder. If I felt like this at the acceptance of the invitation, what was I going to be like at the interview? God knows, I had turned down the invitation several times. But this time I was caught. That bloody Murphy and his big mouth, saying that I was afraid of nothing, and that often I had crossed Mellon's wall after dark. I can hear his words ringing in my ears even now: 'He'll go. Won't you, Yamon, Ya-mon's not afraid. Sure, you're not, Ya-mon?'.

'Okay, Ya-mon,' said Bonker. 'Murphy's a chicken. Are you a chicken, too?' Before I could think, I heard myself saying: 'Okay, Bonker, I'll go'. Now I was stuck with my foolish answer. That bloody Murphy. I wondered what he would say if he really knew how scared I was. Ah, well.

Maybe it would rain on Thursday or Bonker might forget about it.

No such luck. Thursday came and it was the hottest day of the year. As I came out the school gate there was Bonker standing very confidently, smoking a butt of a cigarette. That was real bravery as we wouldn't dare smoke outside the school gate. 'Maybe it is to steady his nerves,' said Murphy. This made me feel a little better. But Murphy was soon gone in the other direction.

'I'd rather be a chicken,' I heard him say as he turned Finnerty's corner.

'Well,' said Bonker, 'are yeh right? Are yeh coming to see the Devil?' We set off together. Hardly a word was spoken until we reached Kilmainham Jail. 'Is it in here?' I asked. I was really scared of the Jail. It was so big and dark looking, with snakes in chains over the door. One side of the Jail is near the Camac River which was full of dirty grey water and rats, rats as big as your arm. I didn't fancy meeting the Devil in those surroundings.

'No,' said Bonker. 'It's not here. But some people say he often appears in that sentry box high up on the side wall. Do you see the box?'

As I looked at the sentry box I noticed that a piece of broken wood, from the roof of the box, was hanging down, making a shadow that looked like a man. It was a sight I wouldn't like to be looking at on a dark night and I was thankful that it was the hottest day of the year.

'Some say that's the Devil,' said Bonker again. 'But it's not my Devil. My fellow is up the road'.

We passed by the Jail, a terrace of houses and the gateway of the Metropolitan Laundry. We crossed the road to Beaconsfield House, which I knew had a fine orchard at the back. 'It couldn't be there,' I said to myself. 'If it were, how strange we never met him all the times we boxed the fox in Beaconsfield House'.

'No,' said Bonker, 'it's here,' pointing to where the Church of St. Jude stood. St. Jude's was a Protestant church and it never seemed to be open. At least, I had never seen it open.

Bonker stood on the footpath, looking in through the church railings. 'It's here,' he whispered. 'It's in that holly bush'.

In the centre of the grounds was a large holly tree. Its green spiked leaves were all stuck together and it was impossible to see into the centre.

'I can't see nothing,' I said.

'Do you not see him? The Devil, I mean?' asked Bonker.

'No,' I said, 'I can't see him'.

'Get down on your knees. Kneel down and then you will see him'.

I got down on my knees.

'You'd better join your hands for protection,' said Bonker. 'Now, can you see him? Can you see the Devil?'

There was I, kneeling down, my hands joined as if I was saying my prayers. I did not notice Bonker moving away but soon I heard him shout: 'Look at that Catholic boy saying prayers in front of a Proddy church. He deserves to see the Devil!'

I got such a fright, kneeling there on my own, that I was unable to get up. But I'll tell you this. I may not have been able to move but my eyes never rested on that holly bush. Bonker soon came back laughing and helped me up off my knees.

About a year later Murphy asked me: 'Did you see the new Devil?' 'What new Devil?' I asked. 'The Devil in the chapel,' said Murphy. I laughed and said: 'Like the other one, I suppose?' 'No. Honest to God,' said Murphy. 'There's a Devil in the chapel'.

So after school, we decided to go down to St. Michael's chapel and see the Devil. When we got to the chapel gate a group of children were shouting: 'I bet ya, I bet ya, ya won't go in and stick your finger in the Devil's mouth. I stuck it in yesterday'.

There, inside the church door, was the Devil himself, as big as life: Horns, fangs, teeth, and the ugliest red face you ever saw. Standing over the Devil was good old St. Michael, with his big spear stuck in old Nick's back.

'I bet ya, I bet ya, ya won't stick your finger in the Devil's mouth'.

Every now and again a little boy would run in and out, shouting: 'I did it. I did it, Johnny'.

The parish priest, Canon Doyle, soon came on the scene. With one wave of his blackthorn walking stick the coast was clear. As everyone scattered the Canon took off his hat, wiped his brow and was heard saying: 'You can't win. You can't win. I spent all my life trying to keep the Devil out of Inchicore and that oul' wan' (the woman who donated the statue) 'brought the Devil into my church'.

12

Cockles and Periwinkles

MA USED SAY that Booterstown was the best spot in Dublin for picking cockles and that the salt sea waters did wonders for her corns. I think Ma was the best cockle picker in the world. As I would say to myself as a child, 'if Molly Malone were alive today, Ma would leave her in the ha'penny place'.

If poor Molly died of a fever she got from her cockles and mussels I bet she didn't pick them at Booterstown. The cockles there were delicious: raw or boiled, I must have eaten millions in my day.

'Never pick a cockle on top of the sand; always ensure they are well under the sand and root them up with your fingers'. These were the orders Ma gave us as we set out cockle-picking. I could never find any under the sand and, when Ma wouldn't be looking I'd pick a few from the top of the sand and throw them into the large shopping bag. Once or twice she caught me and I got a belt on the ear. Then she would show me the marks on the sand and tell me: 'That's how you know where the cockles are'.

But to a child's eyes, all marks and signs on the hot sands under a few inches of water seemed the same, and many's the time I came up with a jelly-fish or a crab instead of a cockle. Ma went out far. Sometimes I thought she was nearly at Howth. But she was always very careful to watch the tide and told us how it comes in and could cut you off on an

island. So, with one eye on the tide and the other on the cockles, she worked to her heart's delight.

When the bag was full we went across to the rocks and had our lunch: the flask of hot tea and plenty of bread and cockle sandwiches, sprinkled with salt and sand. We opened the cockles by putting the end of one cockle into the end of another and giving both cockles a good twist. Ma would take great pains to cut out the part we ate, but we would suck this out with our mouths. I think they tasted better that way: they were much nicer raw than boiled. The only advantage in boiling was that the cockle shells opened themselves. The shells were used for all sorts of games and designs in the back garden. We had so many that they soon lost their attraction and so time and care was taken at Booterstown to find new shells, coloured ones, larger ones and cone-shaped ones. The large cone type was best and if you put one to your ear you could hear the sea, even ten miles away. Collecting these types of shells was an adventure and the Sunday I brought home several large, heart-shaped shells, my pal told me that he had seen them in Woolworth's, being sold at sixpence each as ashtrays.

'How many have ya?' he said. 'Fourteen' — 'That's seven shillings' worth. Are there many more out in Booterstown? All ya need now is the little blue badge with the three white castles to stick on the shells and we have an ashtray factory'.

'Well,' I said, 'not that many. I must have walked miles to find them. But I tell ya what: they say iodine is made out of seaweed and there's tons of it in Booterstown'. I went to bed that night thinking I'd start an iodine factory, but how was I going to get the stuff from Booterstown to Goldenbridge?

The day I saw the man selling cockles and perriwinkles in Moore Street I decided I'd start a cockle factory. I asked him where he got the perriwinkles and he told me that he swam down the Forty Foot at Sandycove for them. He was codding me, of course, and all Ma said was: 'The Forty Foot, me eye'.

We used pins or needles to get the meat out of the small blue perriwinkles but I wasn't all that gone on them and I much preferred the old cockles. Mussels to me then were the big lumps on your arms when you bent your elbow. I was as skinny as a knitting needle, so I wasn't very fond of mussels.

The journey to Booterstown was a joy. The old type trains, which held about 12 people in one carriage, had a door each side and a window which could be pulled up and down by a large leather belt with holes in it. These holes went onto a brass knob so that the window could be opened at whatever length one desired. There were no toilets, so, if one got short-taken, one had to wait until Booterstown.

In the carriage itself was an overhead rack running the length of the seat and the two seats were facing each other. Nearly always some woman in the carriage wanted the windows open and another woman who wanted them closed. If you stuck your head out the window it wasn't long before you got a blast in the eye, a very sore thing, and not even all the cockles in Booterstown would compensate for the bloody blast.

I was a devil for getting a blast and ruined many a Sunday for myself. What I loved about the trains was the six old-fashioned pictures, three on each side of the carriage; brown-coloured prints of the Lakes of Killarney, the Giant's Causeway or the Gap of Dunloe. So, as well as going to Booterstown, I was, in spirit, in all the beautiful places of Ireland.

Another joy about the train was waving to the people in their back gardens and they never failed to wave back. Tara Street Station had only one attraction to pass the time. A large iron machine with a dial of letters and numbers and, for a penny, I could print my name on a piece of metal, pull the lever, set the dial arrow to the letters required and stamp them out, one at a time, by pulling the lever again and again.

The train carriages were marked 'First Class' and 'Third Class' and Ma said that was to show that there were no second class citizens in Dublin. We always travelled third class in carriages full of people while the first class carriages lay empty or with only two or three people in each.

The rush for the train was like the crowd coming out of

Richmond Park football ground, heading for the pubs after the match. The Sunday I caught two crabs, Ma said we will never get home. The station at Booterstown was crowded and two trains had passed by, full to the brim. They didn't even stop.

'Come on,' said Ma, 'we'll get the tram'.

I was furious. I moaned and bawled and not even the two crabs in my little bucket were any consolation.

'The tram. Sure, that's not the way to go home from the seaside. And whoever saw anyone waving 'hello' from the tram?'

But the tram it was, along the swanky Merrion road, with the big houses and tall green trees. I tried to wave but it was in vain. The people on the footpath just looked at me as if I was mad.

It was then I noticed that one of the crabs had made its way onto the big straw hat of the woman sitting in front of me. I was sitting on Ma's knee and resting the bucket on the top of the woman's seat. Now and again she looked over her shoulder at me and she had a very sour face.

I wondered what it would be like if she knew that my crab was having his tea on the coloured flowers of her hat. I tried once or twice to grab the crab but the woman seemed to hold her head higher each time.

When the tram conductor called out 'Merrion Square' the woman and the crab got off the tram.

Coming home from the seaside by the tram was bad, but going to the seaside by the tram was worse than a dose of castor-oil.

I never learned how to make iodine out of seaweed and I found only the occasional heart-shaped shell. I never could learn how to recognise the signs or marks where the cockles lay under the sand, so I never got around to starting an ashtray or iodine factory, or even getting a barrow to sell cockles in Moore Street like Molly Malone.

Maybe I'll learn to swim and go out to the Forty Foot at Sandycove and try my luck at picking perriwinkles. But the water at Booterstown reached only to my ankles and I couldn't learn to swim in that.

Ma wouldn't go anywhere else but Booterstown. She always said 'It's safe, it's nice and it's the best spot in Dublin for cockles'.

13

A Chiseller's Christmas

WE MAY NOT have been able to count the weeks or months to Easter or Whit, or even to St. Patrick's Day, but we always knew when it was only 12 weeks to Christmas. Clarke's sweet and toy shop at the top of Bulfin Road had both windows full of a vast selection of toys. Each item had its own label, telling its own story.

A red fire engine with a yellow ladder: three shillings (or 12 weeks at threepence per week and it's yours on Christmas Eve). A swarm of children, with our noses stuck to the glass window and our warm breaths in the cold October air fogging up the window panes. Then polishing the window with the sleeves of our coats and listening to the chorus of voices all shouting...

'I'm getting that, and that, and maybe I'll get that, but I'm defney getting that'.

Only for Clarke's 12 weeks-to-Christmas plan many's a child in Inchicore and Kilmainham would never have seen a toy on Christmas morning. We seldom missed a Sunday's visit as the shop was only a few paces from St. Michael's Church, and even on a weekday a special visit would be made just to see again the toys we dreamed would be in our stockings at the foot of the bed on Christmas morning.

On Christmas Eve, the girl next door would come in to help me write my letter to Santa Claus. She would dictate the letter and address the envelope, but when she insisted

91

that I put down a blue sports racing car with the number of my hall door (30) on it, I threw down the pencil.

'I want a red fire engine with a yellow ladder,' I said. 'I don't want a blue racing car, even if it has our hall door number on it'.

God bless Bernie, she's a Poor Clare nun today in Belfast, but she had great patience in those days. The battle between the blue racing car and the red fire engine was not won that Christmas Eve as I ran upstairs saying I was going to wait up all night and if Mister Santa Claus tried to off-load his old blue racing car into my stocking I'd give him a good kick.

I remember fighting the sandman that night. The sandman was the man (invisible) who went around at night time throwing sand into your eyes to make you sleep or blind you. But the sandman had won the battle and when I awoke the next morning there was the bloody blue racing car sticking out of my stocking at the end of the bed. I cursed Santa a few times and then noticed the little mouth organ and the sweets in the other stocking. I was told later that this was Santa's way of saying 'sorry', that he must have had only one red fire engine and that he had given it to a poor little boy with no mammy or daddy.

'After all, you have a Mammy, even if you have no Daddy'.

'That's true,' I said and began to think of what my pal had said to me a few days before Christmas: 'You're lucky. You may have no daddy but you have three mammies'. He was referring to my Ma and her two sisters, my aunts who lived with us.

'And besides,' he added, 'mammies are always better than daddies. Sure I never see mine only when he comes home drunk and tries to beat us all up'.

'The Ma and the aunts never get drunk,' I said. 'But I still get bet up, now and again, when I'm bold'.

After Mass that Christmas morning I rushed over to Clarke's toy shop. Both windows were empty. The red fire engine with the yellow ladder was gone. Old Mrs. Clarke, Lord rest her, told me that Santa had collected all the toys last night and she didn't know where the poor little boy lived who had got the fire engine.

I think that was the only Christmas that I was disappointed. The following year I got the red fire engine with the yellow ladder and I wondered if the poor little boy got the blue racing car. I didn't seem to mind what other children got and I never cursed Santa for giving bigger presents to other children. The way I looked at it was, that if you got what you asked for, you were happy.

The twelve weeks to Christmas were spent in joyful mood, singing songs or visiting shop windows or the trip to town to see Santa Claus and climb the stone steps of Nelson's Pillar which was known to me as Corkscrew Alley.

Our favourite song was:

> *Christmas is coming and the goose is getting fat.*
>
> *Please put a penny in the old man's hat.*
>
> *If you haven't a penny, a ha'penny will do.*
>
> *If you haven't a ha'penny, God bless you.*

Then we went to several verses of:

> *Jingle bells, jingle bells, jingle all the way.*
>
> *Hurrah for good old Santa Claus*
>
> *And hurrah for Christmas Day.*

We were well on the streets with the spirit of Christmas long before the real carol singers and musicians appeared.

The shop windows with their white cotton wool made to look like snow: the rows of candied peel, currants, raisins, cherries and all the lovely things for making the plum pudding. The butcher shops with their turkeys and geese hanging from silver hooks. The cake shop with its massive range of Christmas cakes: Oxford Lunches wrapped in silver paper, and the large biscuit tin holder decorated with holly and ivy. Each biscuit tin had a glass lid so that you could see at a glance the variety of cream custard and jam biscuits. Even the hardware stores were decorated with coloured paper chains and the long red Christmas candles were given pride of place in the window. Very few houses had fairy lights or Christmas trees in those days, so we feasted our eyes on the chemist shop window which was aglow in coloured lights, giving new magic to their displays of toilet soaps, manicure sets, combs and brushes. An odd big house on the South Circular Road had a Christmas tree and I stood for hours at the gate, looking at the tree in the window with its coloured lights going on and off every few seconds. The finest sight to my childish eyes was Santa Claus, his reindeer and sleigh of toys in coloured lights high up on the wall above McBirney's shop on Aston Quay or the news coming in white lights along the wall under Lynch's at Burgh Quay. It was magic to watch the news items running down towards Butt Bridge, disappearing and then starting to come on again.

The visit to Santa was made wherever Santa had the cheapest parcels. Prices ranged from sixpence to two shillings. Whatever shop Santa was in, he had his own Toyland, and I've yet to see today anything that could come up to the standard of those childhood years. The view of Henry Street, Earl Street and Dublin City in coloured lights was like Disneyland from the top of Nelson's Pillar.

Helping Ma to mix the plum pudding and being allowed to eat some of the mixture or lick the wooden spoon, then watching it being tied into a white cloth and put into the large black pot to boil... The visits to the kitchen to smell the pudding cooking or watching Ma praising the lovely cake, the bottle of wine and the big red candle, all gifts from Mr. McNamara's grocery shop at Kilmainham Cross.

On Christmas morning we visited friends and relations and tasted their Christmas puddings and drank a glass of lemonade. It was enough to put you off your dinner. Our pudding was always kept for teatime. When it was served and tasted, Ma and the two aunts would say it was lovely, and we'd all agree. After a few slices of pudding Ma and the aunts would hold an inquest on the pudding. They had left it in the pot too long, or too short... too much water or candied peel... it could have done with another bottle of stout.... not enough nutmeg. Despite all this, there was never a crumb left. There were no regulated gas stoves in those days, no tinfoil or fancy recipes. It was made the way Granny made it, tied up in a piece of sheet off one of the beds, known as 'the pudding cloth'.

The old Oblate's Church crib which, unfortunately, was burned to the ground, was one of the best things about Christmas. It had the real atmosphere of Bethlehem. You could smell the stable where the child Jesus was born, see the Three Wise Men in the distance, the angels and shepherds in the semi-darkness, the life-sized figures and the gold thread gowns. The Oblate Fathers in those days brought Bethlehem to Inchicore.

St. Stephen's Day I was up like a lark with my withered branch of a tree, spotted with holly and ivy and coloured streamers and I went from door to door with the Wren Boys. After a few loud knocks on each door we'd sing two verses of the Wren Song:

> *The wren, the wren, the king of all birds.*
>
> *St. Stephen's Day he was caught in the furze.*
>
> *We hushed him up, we hushed him down*
>
> *We hushed him all around the town*
>
> *Roly poly, where's your nest?*
>
> *In the holly and ivy crest.*
>
> *We knock at the door and make the noise*
>
> *For we are the Wren Boys.*
>
> *If you haven't got a penny a ha'penny will do*
>
> *If you haven't got a ha'penny, God bless you.*

The 'God bless' bit was left out and another word put in, particularly if someone roared out of a top window at us to get to hell out of there or he'd send for the Polis.

St. Stephen's Day was the traditional day for a visit to the pantomime in St. Teresa's Hall, Clarendon Street or the old Queen's Theatre in Pearse Street. The coloured chain decora-

95

tions and the cardboard crib were left up for what were known as the 12 days of Christmas and these days always seemed to go slower than the 12 weeks to Christmas. Maybe it was because I was now waiting on my birthday present which came a week after the 12 days of Christmas on January 13.

There were no birthday parties in those days nor were you asked what you wanted for your birthday. It was always a surprise and sometimes it was even better than Santa's present. 'I'm getting this, I'm getting that and that and that, and maybe I'll get that as well...'. The dreams and desires at Clarke's toy shop window were nearly better than the real toys on Christmas morning. I suppose the dreams lasted longer, yes, much longer — they lasted for 12 weeks to Christmas in Dublin.

14

Gur Cake and Coal Blocks

IT WAS a bitter cold Friday afternoon as we stood in the Pioneer Stores waiting to be served — waiting is the right word, we were there nearly a half-hour. The store was crowded. It was like a football match, or as Bonker said, 'Yeh would think they were giving out the stuff for nutin'.

He was nearly too small to be seen and whenever we lifted our feet off the floor we were carried along another few inches to the counter. When the big fat woman was served we plunged forward and reached the cold marble-top counter. We were just in time to see Miss Noone, the cook, carrying the large tin tray of steaming hot Gur Cake straight from the oven to the shop window. Miss Noone took pride in her Gur Cake and we watched her as she arranged it in the centre of the window and then stood there admiring it and sniffing the steam.

'Missus Noone, Missus Noone, give us a ha'pert of that. Ah, go wan Missus Noone, a ha'pert of Gur Cake before it gets cold'.

But Miss Noone, the cook, never served anyone. Her job was to bake the Gur Cake, and she did her job very well. After another few looks and sniffs at her work of art she went back to the cookhouse to get more cake under way. At last we were noticed, not by sight, but by sound.

'A ha'pert of Gur Cake, Miss'.

'You mean fruit cake, We only make fruit cake'.

As we came out of the shop we were stuffing ourselves with the Gur Cake. It was only gorgeous, steaming hot, with sugar-coated pastry and the juice oozing out of the large currants and the other soft brown stuff. We could feel our bellies heating up.

Mr. Howlett, the coal man, was watching us, his eyes poppin' out of his head, as he sat on his coal cart. His jinnett was pulling the cart and shaking its head as if to try and get rid of the coal bell that was tied to its neck, but the higher the jinnett threw its head the louder the bell sounded. Then Mr. Howlett cried out, 'Coal blocks, coal blocks!', and the sound of the bell grew louder and louder. Again Mr. Howlett called, 'Coal blocks, coal blocks,' and we shouted after him, 'What do yeh feed your mother on?' — 'Coal blocks, coal blocks,' Mr. Howlett answered back.

That was the start of our daily winter game with Mr. Howlett. It took a few weeks before Mr. Howlett got browned off with us and started to chase us. That soon stopped the game, as we were dead scared of Mr. Howlett. He looked a nice man on a Sunday when he was all dressed up, but during the week-days he looked terrible angry with his black face and black hands, and the way he wore his cap on the side of his head. 'Coal blocks, coal blocks,' — we'd say nice and soft so that Mr. Howlett would not hear us. 'What do yeh feed your mother on?' 'Coal blocks, coal blocks!' and then Mr. Howlett would add: 'What does yer ol' wan feed yis on? Gur Cake, Gur Cake!' And as he'd roar with laughter, we'd get braver and shout out: 'What do yeh feed your mother on? Coal blocks, coal blocks!' The funny thing is we meant no insult to Mr. Howlett or his good mother. It was all done in fun, with the idea of getting a good chase — innocence and ignorance I suppose, or just plain corner boys!

Yes, we had many chants and sayings then, and some of these can still be heard around Dublin, while others are gone forever like last year's snow.

When a man was drunk we used to say 'he's lackers, langers, twisted, platic, stocious, plastered, pissed, screwed, cross-eyed, elephants, footless, crooked, well-oiled, well jarred, mouldy, under the weather, fond of a drop, a sup on him, he has a little weakness, or he had the failing'. 'I don't think he had a few scoops, he musta had a session'; the man was 'blue mouldy' for the want of a drink and wasn't asked if he had a mouth on him'; 'Well, a bird never flew on wan wing' and 'every dog has his day'; 'God never closed wan door but he opened a half-a-dozen'; 'Him that was bred, born and reared'; 'from all parts and arts' and 'as welcome as the flowers in May in any part of Dublin'; 'A meritless, jeering, sneering lot, that's what yis are, and yer seed, breed and generation were the same. Yis are known to every cat, dog and devil as a beggin' ass — Mickie dazzlers, trying to be Lord Muck'; 'I yask ya, what ails ya, with yer bockety table and yer dirty windows? Remember, fine feathers make fine birds, but ya can't make a silk purse out of a sow's ear — his had never any hand, act or part in antin' that was any good. Night, noon and morning, in hail, rain or snow, yis would rob the cross off an ass's back and if yis didn't get a tin buckshee, yis would put it on the slate and never pay. So now, don't come down near my side of the street or yis will be et, bet and trun up again — et without salt I'm telling yis; any of yous who wouldn't wet the whistle of Shoveler and he blue mouldy for the want of a drink — and no one there to warm the cockles of his heart. Ah well, in the heel of the hunt Shoveler knows his friends, and he doesn't give a tinker's damn about wan of the others'.

When James Joyce wrote his book, *Ulysses,* he asked his publisher, 'How did the book do in America, London and Paris'.

'Sold out, Mr. Joyce, a great success everywhere — well, almost everywhere'.

'What about Dublin?', asked Joyce.

'Oh, Dublin,' said the publisher, 'Well, it's like this Mr. Joyce: in Dublin there are 300,000 people who could have written it better, but they just hadn't got the time to write it'.

'Have you any broken biscuits Mister?' 'Yes,' replied the

shopkeeper. 'Well, mend them Mister!' 'Have you any tripe, Mister?' 'Yes,' replied the butcher. 'Well take the wrinkles out of it mister!'

The new boy starting in the new job was sent for:
— The bucket of steam
— The black and white puddin' bender
— The glass hammer
— The long (wait) weight
— The key of the coal wharf

The above are all in the same tradition as Frank O'Connor's *Bale of Foreskins* which got lost on the railroad between Dublin and Cork. And there is the lady who went in to the Ardee Street pawn shop and put her two big tits on the counter and asked for ten bob on 'government securities'.

I know the old ecker (school exercise) still goes on and I suppose the cog (copying another person's ecker), goes on also. And far too many boys and girls today are out on gur (sleeping rough in the streets or parks), but we as chisellers only made threats of going on the gur. We always seemed to change our minds at night-time.

Another childhood memory of sayings was, 'Eat that up — it will put a red neck on ya'. You'd want to eat an awful lot of gur cake to get a big red neck like a policeman or a farmer, and besides — who the hell wants a red neck!

Another saying which must date back to the famine years was, 'Eat that up or you will follow a crow twelve miles for it!' Old people telling stories had a habit of saying several times during the story, 'Do you follow me now?' As a child I used to wonder where the Granny wanted the Aunt or me Ma to follow her.

'Young blood should never be cold.' I must have heard that a million times during the winter months, as the goose-pimples grew bigger and bigger on me knees and legs between me short pants and stockings that never seemed to stay up, but kept falling down on me black boots.

They tell me gur cake is still made, but it's years and years since I tasted it. I've seen a lot of imposters in cake shop windows, but never anything like Miss Noone's gur cake. Coal blocks too are gone. They appeared when coal went scarce during the Second World War — I think they were more of a dark battleship grey colour than the black coal. Many bellmen made their own coal blocks while others purchased them from merchants of coal block factories. There was a large yard at the Black Lion in Inchicore, and they made coal blocks by the dozen, but the iron-railed gate was always closed, and we never saw coal blocks being made. A money bank stands on the site today, making gold blocks instead.

'Coal blocks, coal blocks, gur cake, gur cake!' Ah go wan, Missus Noone, give us a ha'pert before it gets cold.'

One thing for sure — as long as I live I'll never forget gur cake and coal blocks.

15
Picking Blackers

BLACKBERRY COUNTRY IN Dublin started at the Half-Way House in Walkinstown. All the fields on the left-hand side of the Long Mile Road were laden with blackers. The fields on the right-hand side were laden with golden wheat or oats. The laneway from the Half-Way House to the old Cherry Tree Tavern was lined with sloe bushes and wild Woodbine flowers. The valley from Drimnagh Paper Mills to Lamb's Jam Factory also had its rich crop of blackberry bushes, but the ditches in the valley made it difficult to pick the berries.

Ten minutes' walk from the Half-Way House and the cans, jars, biscuit tins and biscuit barrels and, sometimes, white enamel buckets, were filled to the brim with big juicy blackers. We were sure that no one else in Dublin knew of our secret blackberry fields. Season after season we seemed to be the only pickers around this spot.

Blackberry tarts, jams and even wine which we weren't supposed to drink (but we did) — all were made from the blackers beyond the Half-Way House. The nicest jam in the whole world is pure blackberry jam. Some people mixed apples with the blackberries and ruined the jam: the apple kills the true taste of the blacker.

Hard boiled sweets came in tin cans and the empties were always used in blacker picking. Some people used these cans as milk jugs but the one Mr. Kelly gave me was used solely

for blackers.

A few weeks before picking time we visited our fields, as we called them, to see how the blackers were progressing. While the farmers may have prayed for rain for their crops, we always prayed that there would be no rain, as it spoiled the blackers, filling them with worms or midget flies.

It's funny how the best and biggest blackers always seemed to grow on top of the bush or at a place where the ditch was wide and deep. We didn't seem to mind the thorns sticking in our hands and arms or sometimes scraping our faces as we leaned forward to grasp the fruit. We all thought the poet should have used blackers instead of roses when he said:

> *Ain't this world a funny place*
> *and yet it's hard to beat*
> *with every rose one finds a thorn*
> *but ain't the roses sweet?*

After all, you can only smell or admire roses: you can't eat them. But blackers are different. You can smell them on the bush, admire them better when they are in your can, and you could stay up all night eating blacker jam.

On one of our picking trips one of the gang got greedy and he ran over to a large bush laden with blackers, stretching out his arms, shouting: 'These are all mine, all mine, did ya hear? Go wan off and get your own bush. These are all mine'.

He was standing on the edge of the ditch with his arms out like the shape of a cross. We stood there watching him as he roared again: 'These are all mine'.

'Okay,' we answered. 'You can have them'.

We gave him a push and he fell down into the ditch. It was a deep ditch and he couldn't get out nor could we reach his outstretched hand as he bawled for help.

After half an hour we managed to get him out, he was up to his knees in mud and water. Then we ran like hell from the field. We never allowed him to come with us again. We were sure that it was he who gave away the secret of our blackberry fields because, when the next season came around, an army of children were in the fields before us.

I think he must have told every child in Inchicore and soon the fields at the Half-Way House were bare of blackers. We set out in search of new fields and found a few good ones beyond the Cherry Tree Tavern. But soon these fields, too, became known to others, so we travelled farther down the valley, across the Naas Road to the fields near Bluebell boot polish factory. Everyone now seemed to be in on the act. They were all blackberry jam mad. Then we learned that they were selling the blackers to Lamb's jam factory. No wonder everyone was at it, for there was money in blackers now. We didn't fancy selling ours and not even the price of the pictures to see Buck Jones and Flash Gordon could get us to part with our blackers.

Sure the pictures would be over in a few hours, but the jam would last the week. And thinking of the blackberry tarts on a Sunday or maybe a mouthful of the forbidden wine: no! we wouldn't sell, not even if they paid us £5. Besides, Lamb's wouldn't give us a job picking strawberries in their own fruit fields. The foreman said that he knew by the look of us, that we'd eat more than we'd pick. They could go and fizz off: we were not selling our blackers.

It was David Copperfield who got us to change our minds about selling. There he was, standing in the glass case outside the Inchicore Picture House, the tears rolling down his cheeks like as if he was begging us to come in and see his picture. We couldn't resist. Sure, the whole neighbourhood was talking about the picture. 'Did ya not see it? Did ya not? Ah, ya missed it. It's the best pitcher was ever made'. With all these comments and David's sad face, we decided to sell a bucket of blackers to Lamb's jam factory. Four of us set off to the Bluebell fields to fill the bucket. One of my pals brought his little brother who was about five years old; we were about twelve years of age at the time. We found a fair good field and soon the bottom of the bucket was covered. On and on we picked, filling our little cans and then loading them into the bucket. After a short time we saw that the bucket was nearly full. 'That didn't take too long,' we said.

'Sure we can come back and get another bucketful for ourselves'.

Lamb's factory wasn't too far away, so we made the journey, taking turns at carrying the bucket. We joined the queue at the factory gate. A woman offered us ninepence for the bucket but we would not sell. We needed at least a shilling for three fourpenny tickets to see 'David Copperfield'. The five-year-old wasn't in on the deal and he came along only for the trip. But he insisted that he had helped to fill the bucket and that he was due his share. We laughed at him, but he started to cry, so we decided to try to get one shilling and fourpence for the bucket of blackers. When we got to the weighing scales the man lifted up the bucket.

'How much do you want?' he asked.

'Two shillings,' said we.

'I'll give you one shilling and sixpence,' said the man.

'Okay,' said we, 'wan and six' thinking fast of the twopence extra we'd have to spend on sweets in the picture-house.

'Empty the bucket over there,' said the man, and we tipped the bucket into the big barrel of blackers. Glory be to God! We nearly died. For out of the bucket came not only blackers, but green sloes, leaves and dozens of half-ripe green and red berries (which the five-year-old claimed afterwards were all his picking).

Well, if your man at the scales had looked into the barrel he would have sent for the police. Lucky for us he didn't, so we got paid and flew down the Naas Road. We didn't stop running till we got to the Blackhorse Bridge. It was then we realized that we had left the empty bucket in Lamb's factory. Not all the David Copperfields in the world nor all the blackers in Dublin would get any of us to go back and claim the bucket.

We shared out the money that evening. I held the sixpence for the sweet money and picture money. The five-year-old spent his fourpence on the way home and the little devil wouldn't even give us a sweet or a piece of his liquorice pipe. He said he didn't like pictures. The sixpence nearly burned a hole in my pocket that night but I resisted spending it or entering in the pitch-and-toss school or the pontoon card game at the corner.

The next day, Saturday, we were nearly first in the queue in the dark laneway leading to the Inchicore Cinema. The cash box opened. We got our tickets and sat waiting in the front row of the wooders to make sure no one would block our view of 'David Copperfield'.

The lights went out, the cheering started and on came Wheeler and Wolsey in a funny picture. That ended and the lights went on again. We made for the toilet so that we would not have to go there in the middle of 'David Copperfield'.

The lights went off again to another loud cheer and on came 'Under the Pampas Moon'. We looked at one another and said it must be another short picture. After half an hour we knew it was no short picture and asked the usher when they would be showing 'David Copperfield'. 'Oh,' said the usher, 'that picture finished last night. I think it's gone now to the Feeno on the Quays'.

'Under the Pampas Moon' — sure we didn't see it at all, even though we were in the front row of the wooders. All we could see was David Copperfield's sad face, our blackers, and our bucket in Lamb's jam factory.

A few days later when we saw the sign in the blacker field, 'Beware of the Bull' we moved on to another blacker site and sure wasn't someone building a bloody factory in it, and that was the beginning of the end of our blackberry picking days. We came home with half or three-quarter empty cans and our mouths and faces covered with the red and purple juice of a few blackers which we rubbed on our faces to try and claim that we ate them all on the way home.

'Janey, yis got none — not at all' — but we always said 'Look at our lips, we ate them. They were so good we ate them!'

16

Grand Canal Playground

DESPITE THE dangers, the scares, the warnings, the drowning of others and even the attempts that the Grand Canal made on our young lives, we were always attracted to its banks, locks and muddy green waters. From the first to the second lock it ran parallel to Goldenbridge Avenue. Six roads from the Avenue ended a few feet from the water's edge.

The first road was well named, Suir, after the river, I suppose, because its houses nearly went into the Grand Canal. The second road was named Kickham, which led into Stephen's and O'Leary's Roads, the houses of which stood as if in battle formation, backing up Devoy Road, which flanked the Canal.

The turn at Southern Cross led to Larry the Lockkeeper's house and the Goldenbridge Terrace entrance. The last turn off Goldenbridge was Connolly Avenue and it led just beyond the second lock and a few yards from the old cemetery and Military Road which gave the Canal a ghostly appearance on winter evenings.

Just below the second lock stood Harcourt House, and Mellon's Wall. This was a lovers' lane area — no children allowed — except on the bright evenings when the lovers moved up along the Canal banks beyond the cemetery towards Blackhorse Bridge at the third lock. I would never give a medal to those who designed the foot crossing on the giant wooden locks. They were no more than a narrow plank of wood, held to the lock by large, black, oiled chains; and one had to take great care crossing these footpaths.

Many's the child and adult who tripped over these chains and landed in the water. Many's the time I ran for help and many's the time I saw Peter or Larry fish people out of the Grand Canal.

If certificates for bravery and the saving of lives were given in those years, I'm sure Peter, at the first lock, and Larry, at the second lock, would have been able to wallpaper their houses with these awards.

Wintertime was spent breaking the ice to make a waterway for a family of swans or sitting around a bonfire on the Canal Banks, burning rubber tyres and roasting potatoes. Between the second and third lock stood Brassington's saw-mills with its great big logs and mountains of sawdust. It was there that we learned how to dive and we had plenty of dry swims in the fine sawdust. But the lovely dives into sawdust could never seem to be repeated in the Grand Canal waters.

Beyond Brassington's we had a fine view of the spire and clock of the Oblate Church on Tyrconnell Road. In the quiet of a winter's afternoon the Ave Maria bells had a special sound against the silence of the Grand Canal. The Canal itself had a special sound at every lock. It's waters, too, had a special colour. Gone was the muddy green. In its place, snow white suds jumped up and down as the water slid through the lock like a waterfall. Slowly the barge below in the locks would rise up as the lock space filled to the required level. Then the suds would disappear as the locks opened to allow the barge to take its turf cargo to James's Harbour.

Some barges were horse-drawn and, if the boatman was kind he would allow us to lead the horse along the banks of the Canal, or he might tell us to climb aboard and go down and clean up the galley.

As far as I remember there were always three or four men on each boat. We used take it for granted that the man at the rudder was the captain. We would be disappointed that the boatmen looked like farmers instead of sailors.

The bright blue and white, red and white or all-white yachts that passed through the locks were different. Their captains used wear navy-blue jackets and a real sea captain's cap. Yes, they were a treat to watch, but we were never allowed aboard. Nor were we ever requested to clean up their galleys.

'Where are yiz going?' we'd ask. But our questions were ignored. 'One thing for sure,' my friend would say, 'they're not going for a load of turf'.

'Mister, are yiz going far? Are yiz, mister? Did yiz come from England? Did yiz, mister?' But those aboard the yachts didn't see us or hear us and usually were all business, running up and down the yacht as if they were guiding the vessel through icebergs.

'Sit down, mister,' we'd roar. 'You don't have to do nothing. Peter will open the locks for ya. Peter will do all the work'.

Some families would have their dinner or tea as their yachts were waiting for the locks to fill up. Of all the hundreds of yachts that we saw passing the locks I cannot remember one friendly person aboard. They would not smile, wave or talk and always appeared to us as if they owned the Grand Canal. Despite their unfriendly behaviour we would pay lovely compliments to the colours of the yachts — the flags, bunting and white rope, life-buoys.

'Yer yacht is lovely, mister. Are yiz going far?'

'I like that colour, blue. It's a lovely blue, mister. Isn't it, fellas? Isn't it a lovely blue?'

Then we'd watch the yacht move away and let our eyes follow it as it passed the white thatched cottage of Goldenbridge Farm, the tall green trees at Mellon's Wall, the red gate of Brennan's Dairy and the brown doorway of Parson's paint mills as the yacht reached the second lock.

We would help Peter to close the lock and then feast our eyes on Brennan's milk float coming down the banks of the Canal. The smart brown horse, the polished harness studded with brass; the red-and-white open-back float; two high yellow-spiked wheels, topped by a thin board marked 'Bainne ar dhiol'. The two tall milk churns shining like silver with three bands of gold around each churn, and a gold-plated tap. The large carrying cans with their long spouts onto which were hooked the pint, half-pint and tilley measures. Mr. Brennan standing between the churns in his brown shop-coat.

Our fishing area was along the banks at the rear of Polikoff's clothes factory. This, we learned, was the best spot, as we filled our jam jars with pinkeens and the occasional gudgeon. The white nets were like little bags on the end of a long cane pole. These nets were sold in the shops at a penny each. Later the nets changed colour. Now they were green instead of white and, of course, we were convinced that whoever made the nets had examined the canal, had noted its green waters and had decided to give the pinkeens no chance at all. They might have been able to spot the white nets and slip around them, but would swim into the green net with their eyes wide open.

'The more the pinkeen swims,' we used say, 'the less he sweats'. But no matter what we did or what we fed them, the little pinkeens always would lie dead at the bottom of the jam jar the following morning.

Well aware of this, we often caught a jam jar full, looked at them sadly, then threw them back into the water, saying: 'Go on home. Yer mammy will be looking for ya for yer tea'.

The swimming area at the first lock was under Griffith Bridge or across the far bank which was known as the Shallow. Only the expert swimmers and divers used the lock area. We all regarded the Bogger Griffin as the best swimmer in Dublin. Despite all our practice at diving in Brassington sawmills, we would end up doing belly flappers in the Grand Canal. Sometimes we would chance a jump, an arse-over tip or just climb down the bank into the Shallow.

In summer we were never short of a Saturday night bath. Some children used muck as soap, covering their bodies all over with it and then arse-over tip into the Canal. The young gentlemen, as we called them, brought soap and, of course, one was a great swank if he brought a towel. Usually it was a piece of an old sheet, an old dress or a flour bag. Some just lay on the banks and let the sun do the drying.

There were no fancy bathing togs either. Some got into the water in their short trousers and some got in with no trousers at all. No one seemed to mind as it was a free for all at the Shallow.

Some swimmers could dive in at one side of Griffith Bridge and come up at the other side, all in the dive, with no swimming necessary. My pal, who could not swim, thought this was easy. So in he went and, of course, he came up in the middle and nearly drowned.

When he was pulled out he laughed and said to me: 'Now we are quits, only I did not jump off a bloody boat'.

He was referring to a few weeks previously when I tried to jump off a Canal boat and, instead of landing on the bank, landed in the Canal. Luckily for me, a man happened to be standing at the edge of the bank and, as I was going down for my third and final time, he pulled me out by the hair of my head.

Another man brought me home and claimed that he had saved my life. He got two shillings and a million thanks. I got a million belts of the leather strap, was dried, put to bed and kept in for a week.

The expert swimmers, the fellows who were in the Sea Scouts, were the only ones who dived from the high lock into the Canal. What a sight it was to see them doing the swallow dive or the jack-knife dive. Some of them frightened the life out of us and they swam under-water for ages and came up well away from the locks.

Then the shout would go up: 'There he is, there he is'. A big cheer followed with the usual request: 'Do it again, will ya? Do the swallow again. Ah, go on, do the swallow'.

This seldom failed to get an encore until the evening a man did a jack-knife dive into the Canal and came up with a bucket stuck to his head and blood streaming down his face. But the accident didn't deter the divers. In fact, as the days went by, the number of divers increased and, as everyone now knew the danger, the divers were looked upon with new respect and admiration.

The only thing that got us away from the Grand Canal and its banks was the old Dredger Barge. It cleaned the bottom of the Canal and dumped the soft muck on the Canal banks. Often this stood two foot high on the Devoy Road side of the Canal. The mud was so soft and slimy that it made lovely mud balls. We would make hundreds of these balls and carry them down Kickham Road in box cars or on sheets of galvanized iron and start a mud war with the children off Devoy, O'Leary and Stephen's roads.

I can't say who won the wars as it was impossible not to get an odd belt of a muck ball with dozens of them flying in all directions.

We never learned why they didn't clean the Canal in summer as they would have cut out the muck wars. It would have kept Kickham Road nice and clean and also it would have provided us with plenty of soft muck soap for our Saturday night baths.

17

The Glimmer Man

WE WERE MORE afraid of the Glimmer Man than we were of the war or a German or British invasion. Not even when Lord Haw-Haw, the German radio announcer, said that Ireland, which was the land of saints and scholars, would soon be the land of skulls and crossbones, did we pay any attention to him. Sure, weren't we all ready and organised, right left and centre: gas masks, sand buckets, water hoses, the A.R.P., the L.S.F. and the L.D.F., the 26th Batallion and the Construction Corps.

Every second girl was a Red Cross nurse and the big boys were A.R.P. messengers with real steel helmets and an armband. Oh, we joked about 'Ireland's only hope', but, be jaysus, we were ready. The gas masks were well and truly tested as we stuck our heads down all the street shores. The hoses were used for watering the flowers in the garden and the buckets came in very handy for collecting horse manure around the roads.

A man told us one day that it was the only way we could make money — by following the horses. A bucketful of fresh manure would fetch fourpence from any true gardener. Now and again we ran into a little bit of trouble, when the A.R.P. suddenly called a fire-drill display or exercise and we might have to run from house to house.

'Have ye the bucket, missus?'. 'No, missus, no. The RED bucket, the WAR bucket, the bloody A.R.P. bucket...'. The

117

hose and pump were nearly as bad. It was always lost or lent to someone who forgot who he gave it to. There was the A.R.P. all ready to go into service and we couldn't find the hose and pump. One man came to his door to ask us: 'Did yiz know there's a war on?'. He told us not to be codding ourselves with buckets and hoses. 'If the Jerries drop a bomb here,' he said, 'it's not first-aid, but last aid of holy water and rosary beads yiz will be needing'.

We weren't official A.R.P. messengers: we were too young, but we always moved into the action without being asked. I suppose we were more of a hinderance than a help, but we did manage to find the bucket, hose and pump and believed that we were doing our bit.

I tried to join the A.R.P. messengers but the man sent me home: 'You're too small and skinny and you can't even use a telephone' he said. During the test I put the speaking part to my ear and the hearing part to my mouth. My brother was a messenger and every night he went to bed with his helmet and armband hanging on the bed-post in case of emergency. When I was sure he was asleep I used to get out of bed and put on the steel helmet and armband, look at myself in the wardrobe mirror and then sit at the bedroom window, waiting for German planes to drop bombs. When, however, the bombs fell in the Phoenix Park, the South Circular Road and the North Strand, I was fast asleep in bed.

'Diya know there's a war on?' became the familiar saying as ration books, black bread and a half-ounce of tea per person per week were all you got. The rich people could buy a lot on the black market, but the poor people had to soldier on, on rations. The shop in the Coombe sold a pound of tea for a Pound Note. That was a lot of money to pay in those days and whenever I was sent for it by the lady in the big house, she always gave me sixpence for myself. When I said to the woman in the shop one day: 'It's very dear,' she said: 'Diya know there's a war on, and I had to go to India meself for it!'.

Everything was scarce or rationed. The shortage of petrol brought out horses, donkeys, mules, jinnets and bikes of every description. Some motor vans were run on charcoal and others on gas balloons. The bike or the horse became the safest and surest way of travelling as the charcoal or gas motors were liable to break down without notice. In winter-time, the forge in Dolphin's Barn did a roaring trade, putting frost nails on the horses' hooves. Cigarettes were another problem and the 'No cigarette' sign appeared on many shop counters or windows. 'Get them from under the counter' we'd roar, and run out of the shop banging the door.

Two of the best places for giving out cigarettes to everyone were Brendan Hyland, of Suir Road, and Carthy's, of Errigal Road, Drimnagh. People came from all over Dublin to these two shops to stand in the queue and get their rations on Fridays and Saturdays. Foreign cigarettes began to appear, with all sorts of names: *Yanks, Lucky Strike, State Express, 333* or *555*. Sailors coming into Dublin Port also brought their supply of black Russian, French and Dutch cigarettes, but none were a patch on the old coffin nail *Woodbines* — ten for fourpence or five for twopence. Instead of putting up the price of the tuppeny packet, Wills made a smaller packet and now it was four for twopence; the five packet disappeared. The five Players packet for threepence-ha'penny also disappeared and *Sweet Afton* coupons were no longer free, but cost a ha'penny each and of course cigarette pictures vanished like the snow before the sun.

Air raid shelters were built all over the city. These were long stone huts which later came in handy for courting until they were turned into dry toilets and finally torn down. Newspapers were confined to one page and if anything unusual happened the stop press newspaper appeared. Every-one bought the stop press, but I can't remember any of the reports carried. The A.R.P. issued booklets on how to make your own air raid shelter in the back garden and what to do if an air raid took place. I suppose the rich had their own ones built, but we were told the safest place was in the coal hole under the stairs.

Nearly everyone had a vegetable plot, even the Polo Ground in the Phoenix Park was turned into plots and other parts of the Park were used for coal and turf dumps. Every Sunday, volunteers went to the mountains to cut hard-won turf. The slogan 'Don't close down: switch off' also became a familiar one and the *Dublin Opinion* magazine commented that Radio Eireann should switch off and close down. Gas was also rationed, only to be used at certain peak hours and people were warned not to use the glimmer. The glimmer was a very small jet of gas that came through the pipes during the switch-off period. It would take the glimmer nearly an hour or more to boil a kettle of water. Sure, God love the poor women, dying for a hot cup of *Shell Cocoa, Bovril, Oxo* cube, or tea, if they were lucky enough to have it, and so the Gas Company sent out inspectors to ensure that the gas was not being used during the off-period. These inspectors became known as the Glimmer Men. It was easy at first to spot them, as they all rode Gas Company bikes which were painted orange. You'd see the bikes a mile away. The billy (warning) would go from street to street and road to road— 'Look out, Missus, here's the Glimmer Man'. Buckets of water, wet towels and even the ice and snow in the back garden would be placed on the gas jets to banish the heat, as the Glimmer Men tested the jets by putting their hands on them to see if they felt warm. There must have been many Glimmer Men with burnt hands in Inchicore, Goldenbridge, Kilmainham and other parts of Dublin. Many's the day I kept nix (look-out) for the Glimmer Man. Those who could afford it built little brick fires in their back gardens to boil their kettles and pots, but the vast majority used the glimmer.

One day I was told to stand at the front gate and if I saw the Glimmer Man to rattle the gate latch. After an hour or so a man on a black bike stopped at the gate. 'Where's Anner Road?' he asked. I told him it was the second turn on the right. As he was about to cycle away, he asked me who I was waiting on. I told him I was keeping nix and that if I saw the Glimmer Man I was to rattle the gate latch.

'Well, you can rattle away,' said he, 'because I'm the Glimmer Man'. Just imagine, disguising the bloody bike, painting the orange colour black!

18

Money in a Tin Box

WE WERE sitting on Mellon's wall at the second lock on the Grand Canal, looking in at the big Harcourt House. We were weighing up the lie of the land, to pick the easiest route to the pear and apple trees. Harcourt House was next on our list for boxing the fox.

Over at the house, workmen were building an extension with large red bricks. We agreed that it would be impossible to get in and out of the orchard without being seen by the workmen.

'Come on,' someone said, 'let's go down and box Beacons field again'.

'No, let's box the seven orchards on the High Road or how about the orchard at Islandbridge?'

Just then another voice cried out: 'And what would boys be doing sitting up on a wall like that?'

We quickly turned around, and there he was, right on top of us, a big policeman with his helmet and cloak, the strap of the helmet around his chin and his two arms under the cloak.

I got such a fright I couldn't talk. I was stuck to the wall with fear.

The policeman asked again: 'What are yis doing up on that wall?'

One of me pals saved the situation: 'We're looking for a job,' he said.

'And what sort of a job had you got in mind?' the policeman asked.

'A job carrying the bricks,' said my pal, pointing over to where the workmen were building. The policeman pulled himself up on the wall and looked over at Harcourt House. He recognised the foreman on the job and they exchanged greetings.

'God bless the work, Sean'.

'And you, too, Sergeant,' the foreman replied. 'How are things down at the Barracks?'

'Fair and quiet' the policeman answered. Then he said: 'Sean, the boys here are looking for a job carrying the bricks'.

'Okay,' said Sean, 'Send them over'.

'There ye are, now,' said the policeman. 'I got ye a start. Off ye go and carry the bricks'.

My pals climbed down into the grounds but I was still stuck to the wall. I think I would have remained there but the policeman gave me a little push with his hand.

'Go on,' he said, 'you're going to get a job'.

Three hours later we stood at the corner of Kickham Road, nursing our sick sore hands and cursing the fellow who had said we were looking for a job carrying the bricks, and all for a lousy kid's eye – a threepenny piece!

'Sure that woman over there,' pointing to the house, 'would give you a tanner for going to the chipper in Rialto on a Friday for her'.

'Three one-and-ones'.

'Ah! But that's a message. That's not a job'.

Now carrying those bricks, that was a real job. Yeh, but we didn't get real pay, and I'd rather have a tanner any day than a kid's eye. So there is no difference between going for a message and carrying bricks. The message is easier and you get more money.

But what if you get to the chipper and that cheeky young wan out of Polikoffs is there before you? I'll tell you: you earn your tanner that day, the waiting and waiting and that cheeky young wan sticking her tongue out at you.

Now, if it was a fellow you could give him a dig, but sure

you couldn't hit a young wan. She knew that too, and that's why she used keep sticking out her tongue.

I think the cheeky young wan from Polikoffs used to wait until she'd see us coming. Just as we got to the chipper's door she'd run in to the counter of the shop and say: 'I'm first. I'm first. I'm before them'.

Then her litany would commence: 'Fifty-four singles; seventeen one-and-ones; twelve ray. Have ye any whitenin? Give us eleven; five packets Kerry Blue; four packets Player's Weights; ten packets ten Woodbines and twelve packets five Woodbines'.

Poor Mrs. Pacitti, the owner of the chipper, would be running up and down, punching open the little white chip bags with her fist. Soon a mountain of bags would be all over the inside of the counter.

The silver lids on the fish and chip cooker would go up and down. The large wire mesh pans would dip down into the boiling oil as Mrs. Pacitti's expert eye checked to see if the chips were ready.

From the back kitchen buckets of raw potato chips would be added to the boiling oils. Oh! the waiting, the waiting, and the cheeky young wan sticking out her tongue.

Then the counting of fish and chips, the cigarettes, the checking, the double checking, paying the money in all small change.

It's true, you earned your tanner that day. Sometimes Mrs. Pacitti would try to slip us our order so that we wouldn't have the long delay, but the cheeky young wan would remind her: 'I'm first, I'm first,' and threaten to go elsewhere. And poor Mrs. Pacitti would throw her hands up in the air, nod her head and speak to her daughters in Italian, which we always hoped consisted of a few curses for the cheeky young wan.

'Where else could the young wan have gone?' we asked. 'Pacitti's is the nearest chipper to Polikoffs and it's one of the best chippers in Dublin. You won't catch that young wan going all the way up to Inchicore or down to Cork Street'.

Going for messages for people always paid a halfpenny or

a penny, or you were told: 'Sorry, I've no change'.

Usually we managed to pick up an odd penny or even fourpence for the picture-house. I helped the boy delivering papers for Dowling's shop and he always gave me a kid's eye on a Friday night. I don't know how much he got, but I know I delivered most of the papers.

Then there was Dick the Turf. I liked working for Dick. He was a sight to see, with his orange-coloured, creel-type cart drawn by a big black horse and the load of hand-cut turf, bone dry sods which sold at threepence a dozen. Every sod was the same size, and I doubt if I ever saw any difference between them except that occasionally they were coloured either light brown or dark brown.

We sold the turf from door to door and within a few hours the load vanished. Dick always gave us sixpence each and an armful of turf free. He came every Friday evening, winter and summer. He wore big brown boots and had his trousers tied at the knees with white twine. Wet or fine he never wore an overcoat, just a short jacket, a waistcoat, a black and white striped shirt with no collar and a funny looking soft hat on the back of his head.

He must have been an old man at that time and we cried the day he told us he was going to live with his sister in Waterford, and that we wouldn't see him again.

Peter Ennis from the Liberties gave us a penny each if we helped him to collect slop: pig feed. Peter called it 'waste': 'Any waste, Mam, any waste?' but to us it was slop and it sure smelled like slop.

That was another penny that was well earned. It wasn't too bad if you were sitting on the horse car in front of the big barrels of slop, but, Holy God, if you were sitting behind the barrels on a windy day, you'd need a clothes peg on your nose. After our slop collection someone would say: 'Let's go up to Lamb's factory and smell the jam, or down to Rowntree's factory to smell the chocolate'.

The old Lucan and Merville dairies had a fleet of box-type bicycles selling ice-cream all over Dublin. The 'stop-me-and-buy-one' sign was as familiar as the tram tracks.

The ice cream was packed in a refrigerated container inside the large box. Two tins of wafer biscuits always stood on top of the box. The ice cream man was dressed in a white coat, white hat and white trousers, and he carried in his hand a trumpet-type gold horn which he blew and blew as he came up our road. He would stop at the corner and read our comics while we served the customers. Halfpenny and penny wafers were all the go then. I often sat on the saddle of the box bike, blowing the horn and making up ice-cream wafers with the big wooden spoon and the silver wafer-maker.

For all my work I got a free wafer as well as the thrill of blowing the bugle horn. Then came the day when there were no more wafer biscuits. The halfpenny wafer was gone and the penny wafers were sold in greaseproof paper with no biscuits.

'Sorry. No halfpenny one'.

'Are yiz sold out?'

'No, son, they're not made any more. Only penny wafers, now'.

'Okay. Give us a penny wan'.

'Where's the biscuits?'

'Sorry, son, no biscuits'.

'No biscuits? Here's your lousy wafer. Give me back me penny!'

Soon the word spread. They don't give yeh any biscuits, the mean lousers, and no halfpenny ones. I couldn't stand the abuse, not even for a sit on the bike saddle, a blow of the horn and a free wafer, so I gave up this job.

The war was on, and paper was very scarce, so we turned our attention to collecting waste paper. We travelled all around the streets, keeping Goldenbridge, Inchicore and Kilmainham tidy and filling our sacks with dirty sweet papers, cigarette packets or any type of paper we could lay our hands on.

We sold the paper to the wastepaper merchant in Old Kilmainham. The merchant was a little Jew who inspected and weighed the paper, then gave us a little docket to collect our money, fourpence or sixpence, in the office.

126

On one occasion, as we were on our way to the merchant, a woman asked us if we were collecting waste paper. We told her we were and she gave us a load of lovely clean brown paper which she helped to put into the two sacks on top of the dirty paper.

The little Jew looked into the sacks and said: 'Lovely paper, lovely paper. Put that over with the clean paper,' and he gave us a docket for fivepence each. Of course, when we emptied the sacks, the clean paper was soon covered by all the dirty paper.

The poor little man nearly threw a fit. He ran up and down the yard roaring: 'Dirty paper. Dirty paper'.

After a verbal battle he agreed to pay us fivepence each but we were barred forever from his yard. That ended our wastepaper business.

My next job in door-to-door selling was with Charlie, the orange man. Charlie sold blood oranges at sixpence a dozen. He was a happy, round, tubby type of man who came from the Liberties.

He trained us before we set out on our sales trip: 'Now, lads, always shut the gates and tell each woman that the woman next door is after buying a dozen'.

'Blood oranges, blood oranges,' Charlie would roar from his horse and float car, while we went from door to door. They sold like hot-cross buns on a Good Friday.

'Yes, sixpence a dozen Missus. The woman next door took a dozen...'

This sales talk never failed until I got a house and told the woman the sales story.

'Which woman?' she asked. I pointed to the next house where I had got no answer.

'She bought a dozen, did she?'

Yes, Missus, a dozen'.

'Well, that's very strange,' said the woman, 'because we buried her two months ago'.

Nevertheless, she smiled and bought a dozen. Charlie paid us sixpence and gave us a load of free oranges. If he had no oranges left he gave us a shilling each. That was great money for a few hours' work every Saturday morning. But it didn't last long. Charlie disappeared. All sorts of rumours started: He was dead. The horse was dead. He was in jail. The float was in the pawn. He had lost the horse and float gambling...

Whatever the real story was we never found out. Charlie was gone: he had disappeared, and Saturday after Saturday we waited at Kilmainham crossroads in vain.

One Saturday we waited nearly two hours without a sign of Charlie. When we got back to the corner a young wan met us: 'Where were yiz?' she asked. 'Where were yiz? Mr. Kelly was here looking for yiz to work in his new peanut factory on Emmet Road'.

Within minutes we were at the factory gate.

'Sorry, boys,' said Mr. Kelly. All the jobs are gone. Where were yis when I went looking for ye?'

'Down at the bloody Kilmainham crossroads, waiting for Charlie,' we answered.

If we were disappointed then, we were twice as disappointed that evening as the boys and girls came home from the new peanut factory. All had earned six shillings each. Yes, six shillings each for breaking monkey nuts, rubbing the skin off the nuts with their hands and adding salt, as the nuts were split and put into the roaster.

As soon as I left school I sat for the Post Office examination. I had to pay a half-a-crown entrance fee. A few hundred sat for that exam., for about twenty jobs as messenger boys or telegram boys.

Along with the 279 others I failed so the next step was to sign on for work at the Labour Exchange, beside Liberty Hall. We got no money, but we had to sign on Mondays, Wednesdays and Fridays. At the same time the Ma and the Aunt kept an eye on the 'Situations Vacant' columns in the *Evening Mail.*

As I was signing at the Labour one Friday I was given a green card and told to go after the 'smart boy wanted' job in Trinity Street.

128

KILLEEN AND WESTBY LTD.
TYPISTS & SCRIVENERS
6, TRINITY ST. DUBLIN.

I got to Trinity Street and presented the card to the man in the office.

'You're very small and skinny,' he said. 'Where do you live?'

'In Goldenbridge, Sir,' I answered.

'My God,' he said, 'that's in the country. The job pays only six shillings a week and sure your tram fare would use up at least two shillings. No, I'm sorry, son. We are looking for a boy who lives near the office and you live too far away and you're terribly small and skinny'.

He marked my green card 'not suitable'. The man in the Labour Exchange gave me another green card for another smart boy wanted to serve his time as a cabinet-maker in Moore Lane.

'Mister, where's Moore Lane?' I asked as I met the first man outside the Labour. He sent me in the wrong direction. Another man sent me in another wrong direction. I must have walked Dublin that day looking for Moore Lane. When I finally found it, the gruff man told me the job was gone. I was too late, and he banged the door in my face.

He didn't even look at, or mark, my green card, so I went into a bookie's office and used one of the pencils hanging by twine from the wall and marked the card myself: 'Not suitable'.

When I handed the card back into the Labour, I think the man knew I had filled it in myself. But he was a nice man and he just nodded his head.

Then he said: 'Tell me, son, are yeh trying? Are yeh really trying to get a job? You're very small and skinny. What can you do?'

I told him I could carry bricks and sell blood oranges.

'Okay,' he said, 'Bricks and blood oranges. If I hear anything I'll let you know'.

That night the woman in number 33 Goldenbridge

Avenue, Mrs. Coughlan, Lord rest her, came into our kitchen and said she had a job for me.

'It's only a day's work,' she said, 'But it will keep him off the streets and if he does the day's work each week he will get in on a van in no time'.

My Ma and I thanked her for the job. I was to start at eight a.m. on Saturday morning as the spare van boy with Mr. Stone in the White Heather Laundry. I was to meet the van at Dolphin's Barn Bridge.

On the dot of eight I met Mr. Stone. The van was loaded with parcels and we set off all around Rialto, Crumlin and Inchicore. I was now in my own home area and I knew each road like the back of my hand.

At two p.m. the van was empty and I thought I was finished but Mr. Stone told me to go, get my dinner and meet him again at Dolphin's Barn Bridge at four p.m.

I nearly died when I saw the big van-load of parcels. It was even bigger than the morning load. Stoneybatter, Arbour Hill, Parkgate Street, Islandbridge and Old Kilmainham. It was now eight p.m. Saturday night and only three parcels were left in the van.

'You can drop off here,' said Mr. Stone. 'Don't you live in Goldenbridge?'

'Yes,' I answered. 'But what about my pay?'

'Oh! Your pay,' said Mr. Stone. 'If you call down to the laundry next Friday at four p.m. you will get your pay then'.

I cried all the way home. Next Friday. Sure that was ages away. The Ma told me not to worry as the week would go in quick enough. But to me it was the longest week in my life.

When Friday came at last I knocked on the office window marked 'Inquiries'. The woman in the office heard my story and then handed me a little tin box with my name printed on the lid. She told me to put the empty box into a large type letter box. I opened the tin box and slowly took out the two shilling piece, the threepenny piece and the two black pennies: two shillings and five pence, my first day's pay for ten hours' work!

I clutched the money tightly in my hand, posted the tin

box and ran all the way from the laundry to Kilmainham Crossroads. I sat on the window sill of Jenkin's corner shop, watching all the trams and waiting for Ma to come home from work. I started counting the trams going up and down and when I got to the twenty-seventh tram Ma stepped off.

I jumped down off the window sill and got my usual hug and kiss. I held out my hand, showing her the money, my first day's pay. Ma took the two shilling piece and left me the fivepence for myself. She kissed the two shilling piece. 'For Hansel,' she said and then added: 'That's two shillings off the rent'.

The Saturday work continued for several weeks and then, one Friday I was handed a letter as well as the tin box. The letter told me that I was to start on Monday at seven a.m. The contract was for two years only and the starting salary, fourteen shillings and sixpence a week.

I ran quicker that day to Kilmainham Cross and Ma got off the thirty-fourth tram. I got an extra hug and kiss when she read the letter.

'Now,' I said, 'I will be able to pay the full rent every week because the money in the tin box will be six times greater'.

19

Are you the new Boy?

I WAS standing outside the big brown gate of the White Heather Laundry at ten minutes to seven on a cold September morning, a Monday morning. Across the street Anderson's corner shop clock was barely visible under the weak street lamps. The area was dead silent. An occasional man on a bicycle went up or down the South Circular Road. The laundry building looked dull and the only thing that caught my attention was the iron plate on the wall which read: Sprinkler stop valve system installed.

Across from the gate stood the caretaker's house with its small gate. Suddenly the caretaker appeared. He was a very tall man with a soft felt hat and an overcoat which reached to the top of his brown boots. His name was Mr. Ward.

'Good morning, son,' he said in a friendly manner. That's a hardy bit of a day, isn't it, now?'

'It is, sir,' I said. 'It's very hardy, indeed.'

Mr. Ward opened the wicket gate and disappeared into the laundry, leaving the wicket gate open. I peeped in but I could see nothing, for the place was filled with darkness. 'He seems a nice man,' I said to myself. 'A hardy bit of a day,' it sure was as I looked down at my cold knees and thighs in my short trousers. Even though my old grey overcoat reached to my boots, the wind and cold seemed to be able to run up the coat. I wasn't too bad, really. My head was covered with my school cap and I was well shod. My 'Little Duke' boots had been mended by Mr. Mitchell of Old Kilmainham and he did a fine job on them: two iron heel tips, two iron toe caps and dozens of iron studs on the sole and heel of each boot.

Whenever I scraped my boot off the concrete footpath, red and white sparks flew in all directions. My two hands were stuck in my coat pockets, the right hand resting gently on my lunch, ten large cuts of bread and unsalted margarine — Prairie sandwiches, we called them: Bread and Maggie Ryan, and wide open spaces, meaning there was nothing between the bread except the Maggie Ryan.

My left hand kept apart the 'Baby Power' whiskey bottle filled with milk, standing up straight in the pocket so that it wouldn't spill. At the other side of the bottle stood the small two-way tin, sugar at one end and tea at the other. Now and again my fingers tested the two lids to see that they were secure or felt around the cork on the bottle.

I looked again at Anderson's clock: twenty past seven and not a sign of anyone. 'They must have told me the wrong time' I said to myself, but I'd just have to wait. I took another peep in the wicket gate. This time the lights were on and inside was a large yard, as clean as a whistle, with wooden racks hanging from each side wall like large paintings. There were a few doors along the walls and, at the end of the yard, a small door led to the boiler house. It was a strange sight and there was a strange smell, a mixture of soap, cinders burning, horse manure and the odour that came from our kitchen sink when the aunt was washing clothes.

To me that September morning it was all magic, my new world, a place I'd soon be a part of, knowing every nook and corner. Even if I was a bit shy or cold, I felt good inside and Ma would be delighted to hear all about it, as she loved to talk about her own job as a shirtmaker in McCrea's of Wood Street. From Ma's description I knew McCrea's upside-down and inside-out, even though I never set foot in the place.

Now it was my turn to tell the story and I mustn't forget Anderson's clock, the nice caretaker and the strange smell. As I left the house that morning at 6.30 a.m. the Ma asked me 'What time will you be home at?'

'I don't know,' I said. 'I suppose it will be six or seven o'clock'.

'Never mind, I'll have a stew for your dinner. I'll get Mary to put it on about five. That's the best of a stew,' said Ma, 'the longer it cooks, the better it tastes'.

As I was sort of day-dreaming about my new world, my lunch, and the stew for my dinner, a voice roared out behind me: 'Are you the new boy?'

I nearly fell through the wicket gate with fright. I turned quickly and said: 'Yes, sir. Yes, sir. I'm the new boy.'

'What's yer name?'

'Eamonn Thomas, sir'

'Eamonn Thomas what?' the voice asked again.

'Eamonn Thomas nothing,' I replied. 'It's just Eamonn Thomas'.

'You're a funny fish' the voice said. 'Two Christian names and no surname'.

I don't know whether it was my flat Dublin accent or whether the voice had been to the Abbey Theatre and had seen Sean O'Casey's *Juno and the Paycock* but there and then he christened me 'Joxer'.

'I don't like calling boys by their surnames,' the voice said, 'and Eamonn doesn't sound right for a van boy. So I'll call ya 'Joxer'.'

I began to think then that he didn't like de Valera and he didn't fancy having to use one of Dev's names to order a van boy around.

The voice came from another tall man. He was not as big as Mr. Ward, the caretaker, but he was a fair height. He was dressed in a smart blue suit, soft grey felt hat, and he had a brown leather cash bag hanging at his right side. I noticed that the leather strap of the cash bag hung across his chest and left shoulder and was lightly polished. He wore a white shirt, stiff shiny collar, and plain blue tie. His shoes were black and gleaming. On his left arm he carried a heavy grey overcoat.

'I'm George,' he said. 'George Dormer, your new van

134

man.'

'Hello, George,' I said, putting out my hand to shake his. He shook hands but I knew by the look he gave me that he didn't like the idea of my calling him George. A minute's cold silence passed. Then he said: 'Tiny will be here in a minute. The devil's always late. He'll show you what to do'.

We both stepped in by the wicket gateway. He went into one of the side rooms and told me to stand at the wall racks.

'That's our spot,' he said. 'Tiny will show you the ropes'.

Ten minutes later Tiny arrived, puffing and panting as if he was after running miles to the job.

'Is he in yet?' he asked me as he puffed and panted and held his chest with one hand.

'Do you mean George?' I asked.

'Jaysus, don't let him hear you calling him George or you'll put him in bad humour for a bloody month,' said Tiny.

'What do we call him?' I asked.

'Mister Dormer, to his face, and the ol' bollox, behind his back!'

We both laughed.

'Come on,' he said, 'and I'll show you the ropes'.

He told me his name was Tommy, but George insisted on calling him Tiny, and he didn't like the nickname.

'What's he going to call you? — It won't be Eamonn, that's for sure'.

'No,' I said. 'It's Joxer'.

He laughed. 'That's funny,' he said.

Although Tiny was much bigger than me, I told him there and then that I didn't like the nickname 'Joxer' and that if he laughed again, I'd give him a dig in the nose.

Tiny's eyes went sad.

'Okay,' he said, 'I'm sorry'.

Both of us made a deal not to call each other by those nicknames and, from that day on, we worked happily together.

Show ya the ropes... Ropes were the only thing I didn't

see. The tour commenced in the laundry. This is the sorting room where the girls put the customers' numbers on the clothes with pens and special ink.

'Miss Webster is the nicest girl in here. You must know her brother, he plays goalie for the Gate'.

Our taste in girls was identical. To me, also, Miss Webster was the nicest girl.

'This here is the packing bay. That's the ironing section. Miss McGill is the best ironer in Dublin — that's her table'.

All the ironing was done by hand with small silver steam irons.

'The best place is the wash-house,' he said. 'Come on, it's up here'.

The wash-house was at the rere of the laundry: large wooden tubs, tanks and open wash basins like a large swimming pool. The women in the wash-house wore wooden clogs, rubber aprons and worked in pairs washing blankets and sheets by hand in the large tubs and baths, with their sleeves rolled up and their backs bent over their work. Now and again they withdrew their red arms which were covered with soap suds. The women in the wash-house were the oldest women working in the laundry. Nearly all of them had snow white hair, tied up in buns at the back of their necks. They came in at six a.m. so that they could have work ready for the girls who started at 8 a.m. I was fascinated and ashamed watching them, as I had never seen women work so hard in all my life, and I was glad that the Ma worked in a shirt factory.

Next to the wash-house was the drying room and the large hand-operated mangles. Everywhere there were large wicker creels on ball racer wheels for taking the clothes from one spot to another on their journey around the laundry. These creels were as light as a feather, and they glided along the stone floors. The heavier the load, the quicker the creels travelled.

'That's it,' he said. 'Oh, and that's the office door. Miss Rudd is the boss. We hardly ever see the big boss, Paisley. Miss Rudd runs the joint. That's where you get paid on a

Friday. They make out all the bills and take in the money. Come on, now, and I'll show you the boiler house and the stables'.

In the boiler house I was given an empty bucket and told to go and ask the boiler man for a bucket of steam to wash the horse's feet.

The boiler man was very nice, and he told me gently that they were fooling me. While Tiny and his friends were outside laughing I was given a private tour of the boiler house and told about steam pressures, gauge clocks, coal, coke, cinders and the way they kept the tall chimney clean. The stables were next. That's the harness room.

'That is the oats bin. Note how it's locked. That's in case we steal an extra bucket of oats for our horses. But I know how to pick the padlock and get an odd extra bucketful. The two end stables are ours. We have two horses, Daisy and Sergeant'.

'In the morning, the first thing you do is let out Daisy for a drink, clean out her stable, put in fresh straw for the bedding and lock the stable door. We use Daisy on a Monday, so we have to bring a bucket of water to Sergeant and clean out his stable while he's still in it. Give him a bucket of oats and that's that'.

'The next thing we do is currycomb and brush Daisy, oil her hooves, put on the harness and give her the nosebag. On Thursdays we oil and brasso the harness and wash the van'.

Then I got my first lesson in harnessing a horse. I was so small and Daisy was so tall, that I had to stand on a two-foot wooden log to do the job. Tiny insisted that the best way to learn was to do it yourself. I was scared stiff of Daisy. Sergeant was a quiet old horse, and he would nearly help me to clean his stable or indicate with his nose a piece of manure that I had overlooked in my fear, and he always moved around the stable to make sure he was out of my way.

Tiny told me that Sergeant was afraid of the fork and was helpful in case you might stick it in him. Tiny also told me that the horses had special magnifying eyes which made the

horse think that we were giants. After those few encouraging
words I was never again afraid of horses, but Daisy, being a
girl horse was always very difficult to manage. The first
thing on was the collar. Just as I had it in position Daisy
would throw up her head and scatter the collar and me off
the wooden log. After a few attempts I got the collar on.
Next was the reins which fitted into the collar. The straddle
was easy to put on but it weighed a lot. Next on were the
horse's blinkers, bridle and the iron bit into Daisy's mouth.
This was another hard job as Daisy kept her teeth firmly
together to prevent the bit entering her mouth. Tiny showed
me the part of her mouth to press, and soon the gate of big
teeth opened wide and the job was done.

Next was to back Daisy in between the shafts into
position, hook on the traces and secure the belly band and
reins. It was now eight-thirty a.m. and George appeared to
tell us we were half an hour late and that we would have to
pull our socks up.

I don't know why he said that as he couldn't see my socks
under my long overcoat, and Tiny wore long trousers.

George checked the horse, the harness, the van. 'Okay,'
he said, 'up you go, Tiny and Joxer'.

Tiny said the senior boy always sat on the outside so I
was now sitting on a plank of wood that acted as a seat at
the front of the two-wheeled van. George was on my right
with a cushion on his part of the seat. Tiny was on my left
on another cushion, and I was in the middle on the bare
board. In front of me was an iron bar rising up to hold the
tarpaulin cover which was tied up like the sail of a ship along
a wooden beam which ran the length of the van. Just in front
of my face was Daisy's tail and backside, and the smell of
her farts as she went out the laundry gate and headed for
Cork Street.

I liked the sound of the van wheels and Daisy's hooves on
the grey-black cobble-stones. The air was cold on my face
but the sun was trying to break through the clouds, and
George said it wouldn't rain.

From my high seat, Cork Street looked very well, and I

felt important as we waved good morning to the other horse vans. Now and again George would raise his hat as a woman or girl smiled or said hello.

Fourteen hours later there were no smiles, no waving hello, no raising of hats, but Cork Street still looked beautiful in its blue and green gas lamps — beautiful to me, anyway, as I knew the laundry was only around the corner, and within another hour I'd be having my dinner of stew, as the Ma said 'the longer it cooks the nicer it tastes'. Tonight it was going to be the nicest-tasting stew in the world, but how was I going to remember all the stories for Ma?

20

A Lovely Dublin Stew

IT WAS WELL past midnight when I finished the stew. Ma was crying and saying the hours were terrible long, and I was so thin and small, and asking me to give it up, look for another job, only two shillings and five pence for all that work and time. She nearly had me sobbing too, but I told her about the laundry, the bucket of steam, the vanman's two names, the washerwomen in the clogs and rubber aprons and about the horse helping me to clean the stable.

Soon we were both laughing, and we agreed that if I felt like giving up the job I'd tell George where to put his van and his horse. But, as I went to bed that night, I knew I would never give up the job. It was the rent for Ma and I knew she was very proud of me, and she loved the way I told the stories.

The laundry route took me to nearly every street, road, lane and alley on the north side of Dublin. The dirty clothes collected on Monday were delivered fresh and clean on Thursday and Friday. Tuesday's collection was delivered on Saturday. Wednesday was a special day, the country run. We collected and delivered at the same time. I felt like Aladdin, but instead of giving new lamps for old, I was giving new, clean clothes for the old and dirty, provided, of course, that the customers paid their bills.

'Five and ninepence from yer woman,' George would say, 'and don't leave the parcel 'til she pays ya'.

George didn't talk much except when he was complaining. He was a widower, left with a few small children, but he always seemed to me to be a very lonely man. He was very strict, very dour at times, had very little sense of humour, but he did have integrity. He never used a vulgar word and, despite all his complaining, he always gave me sixpence every Saturday night for 'being a good boy'. Yet he never praised me during the week, but I noticed a few times that he trusted Tiny and myself, and often left his bag of money with us while he went to the toilet.

George was very popular with the customers, and was a pillar of the White Heather Laundry. We seldom had a customer's complaint. Once in a blue moon someone would lose a tablecloth or get the wrong shirt, and George himself would search the laundry high and low to rectify the mistake.

The Monday collection started at Eden Quay and around by the old Liberty Hall to Amiens Street. It was in this street on the first Monday morning that I nearly lost my job. George pointed out the two houses and gave me the bills to collect the money. As I got to the door of the first house I saw it had an old-fashioned knocker, a man's face with a long beard. I caught the beard of the knocker and gave three loud knocks. Within seconds I gave another four loud knocks and I was going to have another go at the beard when the door opened.

'Who are you? How dare you knock on my door like that! Who are you? I'll get you sacked'.

I stood there with the green bill in my hand. I was more scared of this woman than I was of Daisy the horse.

'I'll phone the laundry now and get you sacked'.

'Please, Missus, don't get me sacked. This is my first day on the job. I'm sorry I knocked too loud. It won't happen again. Please, Missus'.

She looked down at me over her silver-rimmed glasses and then again under them. Finally, she took off the glasses and looked at me again.

'I'll give you another chance,' she said and then she showed me how to knock on a door. She put her hand around your man's mouth and gave two little taps.

'That is how you knock on a door,' she said.

She paid the bill, gave me another bundle of laundry and said: 'Good morning. Don't forget to close the gate'.

The second house had the same type of knocker, so gently I took the beard and gave two little taps. I waited a long time before I gave another two little taps, and after another long pause still no answer.

I looked across at George and he shook his fist up and down a few times, indicating that I should knock harder.

I tried one loud knock: still no answer. As I was about to leave, the woman of the house looked out the window, saw me, waved me back and then opened the door.

'I didn't hear you knocking,' she said. When I told her I had knocked three times, she said: 'Ah, you don't know how to knock on a door. This is the way you do it'.

She grabbed the beard and gave five loud bangs even louder than the ones that nearly got me sacked. I told her about the woman a few doors away.

'Don't mind that ol' wan,' she said. 'If she was deaf like me she'd know all about it'.

As I closed her garden gate it struck me that Tiny never had shown me the ropes. But how could George see my socks? 'Pull up your socks,' he roared across the street. But ropes and socks didn't matter much. My worry now was how to knock on a door.

The van turned at the Five Lamps and we collected as we went along Seville Place, Sheriff Street, Castleforbes Soap Works and into Caldon Road: then the three Gilna shops, house by house to Church Road, Moyalta Road, down to Fry Cadbury's, Merchants' Road and on by the gate to Alexandra Basin.

The gate policeman gave us a ticket out of his big thick book. George stuck the ticket into the cash bag and soon I was in the lift of the Dublin Port Milling Co., going to the top of the house to collect a basket of white shop coats. The man had to stand on the coats to get the big basket closed.

'How, in the name of James's Street, is a little fellow like

145

you going to carry that basket?' he asked.

'I don't know, Mister, but I'll try,' I said. He gave me a hand to get it up on my shoulder. It cut into my skin as I balanced it and I staggered to the lift. Down I went, my knees buckling under the weight. When the lift stopped and the gate opened George's eyes nearly fell out of his head.

'Are ye trying to kill yourself?' he roared as he lifted the basket off my shoulder.

A few more stops along the road, then back again to the gate policeman. The ticket was returned, marked and timed and we were allowed out.

Back up East Wall to Leinster Avenue, Nottingham Street, the North Strand and Scott's Jam Factory where I was told I could buy a two-pound pot of strawberry jam for tenpence. (At that time it was one-and-ninepence in the shops). So every Monday it was three two-pound pots of jam — one for George, one for Tiny and one for me. That was real strawberry jam, with a dozen or more strawberries in each jar.

But all good things come to an end and when Scott's started exporting the strawberry jam to England they would sell us only apricot, which was threepence dearer (one-and-a-penny a jar). The apricot jam was like water; you could pour it on your bread, or spread it on with a paint-brush.

'Apricots,' the Ma would say, 'It tastes more like turnips'.

From Scott's it was over Annesley Bridge, Cadogan Road, Philipsburgh Avenue and every road in Marino, across the Malahide Road and down to Clontarf Railway Station.

At Hollybrook Road I was given a sack and another few bills and told that the houses were in front of me on the Howth Road and that I was to walk down St. Lawrence's Road and there meet the van again.

I had no trouble with the first two houses but at the third I was stopped by a policeman who examined the sack I had the laundry parcels in. My name and address were taken. The laundry bills were examined closely and then I was allowed in the gate. Two more plain-clothes policemen examined the sack of laundry and I was allowed on my way. When I told all this to the woman in the house, she said they

146

were protecting Mr. Boland.

Well, I met the van and soon met Furry Park and Dunluce Road where the nice woman boiled the can of tea for us and we 'drummed up' — had our lunch on the footpath of Dunluce Road.

The iron bit came out of Daisy's mouth. The nosebag went on her head and then we sat down to our billycan of tea. George loaned me his cup, but warned me to bring me own the next day. Tiny was drinking out of a jam jar. 'Tin cans made the tea too hot,' he said. We got two cups of tea each and I ate all my bread. It was now almost one o'clock and the van was packed with dirty laundry.

The lunch break lasted about twenty minutes. Then I was sent off with Tiny and two sacks and a bundle of bills. Tiny told me that George would look after Daisy, would make a few calls on his own and meet us at the end of Mount Prospect Avenue. Away we went. Castle Avenue, Seafield Road, Kincora Road, Vernon Grove, Sea Park, Mount Prospect, Dollymount and St. Anne's, and back to the end of Prospect Avenue to meet George, and Daisy.

St. Anne's estate was like the country with its trees, wild flowers and birds. Tiny said it was haunted at night. As the van made its way along the coast road I had a fine view of Howth and Dalkey. 'We must be nearly finished,' I said to myself. 'The van won't hold much more and it's nearly three o'clock. With a bit of luck I'll be home about six'.

Haddon Road and Clontarf Castle were the next stops and then back to the coast road with a fine view of the big gasometers and the oil tanks.

'That's it,' said George, as we went under Clontarf Bridge. 'We're finished,' I told myself again. 'I'll be home at six'. We were nearly on top of it before I saw it: an empty White Heather laundry van with Sergeant, the horse, drawing it.

'Is he only starting out now?' I asked. Tiny and George laughed and said nothing. The two vans came side by side.

'Hello, George, that's a good load you have. Is he the new boy?'

'Hello, Paddy. Yes, it's a fair load and he's the new boy'.

147

'Right,' said Tiny, 'change here for the Cat and Cage'.

I nearly cried as I sat in the empty van and watched Paddy Norton drive off with our van-load of laundry and Daisy.

I tried to make up the number of hours it had taken us to fill the first van. Surely we would not have to fill this one as well? Donnycarney, Artane, which was then only a village with a pub, a blacksmith's forge and a few cottages. Back again to Belton Park, Collins Avenue and Celtic Park. The rest of the area consisted of fields. Down Gracepark Road, into Griffith Avenue. Back down to Glendore Road, which was then a dead end, with only a few houses. Up to Calderwood Avenue, which was also a dead end and which was known as Goose Green.

The next stop was the Gaeltacht, which the area in and around Iveragh Road was known as. Around Larkhill Road, with the old tin church in the middle of it; the rest was fields. Down again to Griffith Avenue and up and down Clare, Lambay, Rathlin, Homefarm, Arran and Achill, Ferguson, O'Daly, Walsh, Fleming and Hardibeck Roads.

Under the street lamp outside McCarthy's public house George added up his book and counted the money in the brown leather cash bag. Tiny and I were sent off with another two sacks and more bills. The first stop was Ferndene, the next the Cat and Cage, Ormond Road and Clonturk Park, which was also a dead end.

Back up to the corner of Clonturk Park where the old Drumcondra Grand Cinema stood. Tiny and I discussed the picture they were showing. Yes, we both had seen it: 'The Roaring Twenties', and as we looked at the film-stills in the two glass-cases we'd say to each other: 'Do you remember this part? That was where he was killed in the end'.

'No, I don't remember seeing that part,' as we looked at another still which, probably was cut by the censor.

Across the road to Millmount Place and back again, across the road to Richmond Road, down as far as Tolka Park and then over to Hollybank Road, to meet the van. On again to Dargle, Alphonsus, Patrick's, Anne's, Whitworth, Wigan, Claude, David and Drumcondra Hospital, where a few patients were lying out in the open with only a roof over their heads. Then Fitzroy Avenue, Jones's Roads, the Clonliffe, Ballybough and Summerhill. The shop I liked best in Dublin was Stein's, pork butchers, in Parnell Street, because that was the last stop on a Monday night.

As soon as we got back to the laundry yard, we unloaded the van into the wicker creels and pushed them neatly into the sorting room. In the heat of the sorting room the black clocks (cockroaches) would be running around the floor in their hundreds. I suppose that was the biological way of eating the dirt out in those days!

While George went into a room to count his money and put his book in order, we unyoked the horse, took off the sweat-smelling harness and led the horse to his stable.

It was twenty minutes past eleven by Anderson's clock as I came out of the laundry gate and I was due back in at eight a.m. on Tuesday morning. While waiting at the bus stop for the last bus it struck me that we didn't stop for tea, and suddenly I became very hungry, tired and cold.

The bus conductor gave out to me for being out so late at night.

'You ought to be ashamed of yourself,' he said, 'staying out this late. I suppose your poor mother is worried stiff'.

'I suppose she is,' I said, 'but I'm not ashamed. I'm very proud. I'm coming from work'.

He just looked at me, nodded his head and said: 'A laundry boy'.

'Yes,' I replied, 'I'm a laundry van boy and I'm going home for a lovely feed of Dublin stew!'

21

Paying the Rent

THE FOLLOWING morning, Tuesday, I awoke at seven a.m.
It was about five minutes to eight as I was entering the
laundry wicket gate. Tiny had told me the night before that
Daisy rested all day Tuesday and, if I got into work before
him, I was to clean out and yoke Sergeant. Unlike Daisy,
Sergeant held down his head to allow me to put on the collar
and harness. Maybe Sergeant hadn't special eyes and he
could really see how small I was and took pity on me.

Tiny came puffing and panting at ten past eight and
George let his roar up the stable yard five minutes later.

At eight-thirty we were driving down Cork Street. Our
first stop was Church Street and every street, road and lane,
left and right, out as far as the Albert Agricultural College
and the ten red bricked Wadelai houses on the far side. The
rest was fields, except for Stormstown House, Clonmel Farm
and Pappinstown, with its old church and few whitewashed
cottages.

We came back down Ballymun Road into Cremore Drive
and passed more fields, then down by the Holy Faith
Convent to the Washerwoman Hall. We called to a little shop
with a big sign outside the door: 'Smoke Mick McQuaid
Tobacco'.

A few doors away stood Delville House where the Bon
Secours Hospital stands today. At the foot of the hill, beside
the Tolka River, stood the old tin or wooden church and,

next to it, an old school, known locally as the Ink Bottle. Then on to Botanic Avenue, with its nice white houses where the workers of the John Player factory lived.

Michaels, Malachy, Daneswell, Fairfield and Marguerite, to collect the large basket in John Player's works.

'Will you sell us five Player's Weights cigarettes, Mister?' we asked, thinking they might give us a few for nothing. But we never got a butt, not even at Christmas time.

Another large basket was collected from Alex Thom's Printing Works, then down Iona and up Lindsay Road, and my first visit to The Brian Boru public house where I got a nice drink of water while I was waiting for them to parcel up the laundry.

Beirne's shop opposite was next. By this time the van was nearly full and it was two p.m. by Doyle's clock on the corner of the North Circular Road. At this stage I was watching out for empty White Heather vans but there were none in sight and soon we were back down Church Street, up the Quays and over Queen Street Bridge to Bridgefoot Street, Pimlico and Marrowbone Lane, and into Cork Street.

'We dine in the laundry today,' said George. 'Did ya bring a cup?'

'Yes,' I said, as I took my fancy mug out of my overcoat pocket.

George and Tiny laughed when they saw the mug which had a swan sitting on the front of it.

'Where did ya get a thing like that?' George asked.

'I got it with an Easter egg in it, when I was at school in Basin Lane. Me Ma was keepin' it in the china cabinet but she let me take it to work'.

I was annoyed at them jeering my mug. I was very proud of that mug which I won in Sister Monica's class. But I must admit it did look funny beside Tiny's jam jar and George's enamel mug.

The swan's neck was up over the top of the mug and he was facing out. Tiny said the swan would break his neck if he ever tried to turn and drink out of the mug. In the laundry there was more laughter as everyone was brought in to see

152

my funny mug.

All the other boys were drinking out of tin mugs, the lids of billycans or jam jars. Some of the laundry girls said it was a lovely mug and not to mind them as they were jealous and hadn't one like it.

After lunch, Tiny brought me into the laundry to meet Miss Webster and chat up the girls. Afterwards he asked me which mot did I like the best so, to be on the safe side, I said they were all very nice.

I didn't tell him that the redhead from Rialto Street and the dark one with the brown eyes from Maryland were my two favourites on the packing benches, and that I promised to help them stick the labels on the parcels on Thursday and Saturday.

At four p.m. we left the laundry again. The first stop was the priest's house on Arran Quay. Next, Duggan's, the draper's shop, then the Sligo Hotel, where I collected about nine parcels, and on to the old Four Courts Hotel, which always had the smell of an orchard. I think they used fruit flavour polish but it was as quiet as a church and four parcels were collected. Beside the Four Courts Hotel was the barber's shop stop and then, around the corner we went into Morgan Place, where a nice old woman living on the top of a tenement house gave me a small parcel. Around by Chancery Place and into the Four Courts building, down to the apartments of Mr. Woods. No one seemed to mind me or question me as I explored the Four Courts, looking for Mr. Woods' door. He was a nice friendly man and always gave me a smile and a few words.

He treated me as if I was a friend calling, instead of a laundry van boy. I think this was one of the things that made the job interesting. Nearly all the customers were very friendly and cheerful. It was only the small few who looked down their noses and made it seem like a favour that they were allowing me to carry their dirty shifts and shirts or tea-stained table-cloths.

Ormond Quay, Chancery Street to Mary's Abbey and Murphy's Wholesale Grocers. The man in Murphy's looked dumbfounded and he explained to me that he was sorry for keeping me waiting but that a nun had just left with a bottle of whiskey among her groceries and that the nun had told him to put the whiskey down on the bill as butter.

'Well, God bless her,' he said, 'if it's for an old man or woman: and God bless her twice if she's drinking it herself'.

Capel Street and the city centre to 37 Parnell Square, where John McCormack sang his songs for Dr. Vincent O'Brien when McCormack was nothing. At least that's what the woman told me when she opened the door.

Granby Lane, where I knelt at the little altar to Matt Talbot and said a special prayer for Ma. Over then to the Belvedere Hotel and James Joyce's School (Belvedere College), the Georgian Squares, Dorset Street, Derrynane, Innisfallen, the Mountjoy Prison warders' cottages. Eccles Street to Fontenoy Street. Back to Berkeley Road, Goldsmith Street and Dalymount, the Navan Road, Great Western Square and Rathdown Road to Grangegorman: it looked a very dreary place in the weak gas lamps on a winter's night and I was glad we had no stops near it.

Smithfield and Queen Street — the last stop was Keogh's, the undertakers, and it too, was dreary as I made my way through the workshop of coffins to collect the laundry. Even though the coffins were empty, some half-made, not even varnished, they still gave me the creeps until the Saturday I saw a workman eating his lunch and drinking his tea out of a coffin. I was never afraid again.

We got back to the laundry at nine p.m. George told us to go home: he would do all the rest of the work himself but we were not to forget the next day was Wednesday and that we would be due in at 7 a.m.

Wednesday morning was wet and windy as I made my way down Rialto to the laundry yard. I reached the gate at seven sharp. My coat and cap were wringing wet and the boiler man told me that he would dry them in the boiler house after I had dealt with the horses and when I was inside the laundry, loading the van.

I wasn't too fussy currycombing Daisy or oiling her hooves

155

as the rain was now falling in bucketfuls. Tiny was late again and George was getting the wall racks ready to sort out the laundry parcels.

When I brought in the horse and van George explained how the sorting system worked. The secret of the trade is sorting bills, he said; and the sorting of parcels is the secret of the load. Soon I was to know both secrets but George wasn't too pleased when he found out that I could sort the bills and the parcels and name all the roads and places, one after another, off by heart.

That first Wednesday morning George told me where to put each parcel and basket. He sat up on the van and, as I read out the label, names and addresses, George pointed out the appropriate place on the racks. We had nearly half the parcels sorted when Tiny came in, puffing, panting and wringing wet. George ignored him and continued to give me instructions. As soon as all the parcels and baskets were in place, George started loading the van. We worked off the racks from left to right, starting with the floor rack and moving up until we reached the fifth and final one.

Loading the van was a work of art, as the parcels and baskets formed a wall high over both sides. The tarpaulin cover was drawn down over the load and tied to the sides of the van and the iron bar that was in front of my seat.

The boiler man brought me out my coat and cap, both bone dry. I thanked him, put them on, lifted the lunch basket into the van, checked that we had the nosebag, the side lamps, spare candles and, as the factory hooters were blowing for eight bells, Daisy was trotting down the South Circular Road, heading for Islandbridge.

We turned left at the Phoenix Park's swinging gates and the first stop was at the King's House, Chapelizod. By this time the coat and cap were just as wet as they had been before the boilerman dried them.

A few stops in the village and on to Palmerstown, which was then wide-open country, with only a few big houses, a racing stables, white thatch cottages, the new bungalow of the doctor of Stewart's Institution and the old Institution itself. Beyond it, a pub, a forge, a small shop, a few cottages and wide-open spaces.

Next stop was The Dead Man's Inn and two big houses opposite and the old Lucan tram sheds with tall chimney and broken trams; Ballydowd and Father Hooke's House at Lucan Church. I thought it was terrible for such a nice priest to have a name like Hooke, but he didn't seem to mind and I suppose he couldn't do anything about it anyway. But, to me, a hook was a crook, and a priest shouldn't have a name like that.

Down, then, we went to Giltrap's shops which were everywhere, and up the hill to Sarsfield's demesne at Lucan.

'Oh! that this were for Ireland,' I cried as I handed in the parcel but the gate lodge keeper wasn't impressed by my historical knowledge of Patrick Sarsfield. He grunted and said 'How much do I owe ya?'.

Lucan Lodge was next, and on to the old Spa Hotel, which was more like a private hospital in those days. Men and women in wheel chairs with white-coated male and female nurses. The grounds were strictly private and I had to open and shut the large iron gates at the entrance. It was a place where no one seemed to speak and to me the people in the wheel chairs gave the impression, by their faces and manner, that they were suffering great pain.

Next, the Hermitage, and then not another stop until we crossed the Salmon Leap Bridge at Leixlip. Shakleton's tall, large house, covered with ivy... Roly Daniel's Road Show which camped its blue and white caravans in a field beyond the bridge... Wardell's, the Mall, Leixlip Castle and the public house. George gave me fourpence and told me to buy him ten Woodbine cigarettes in the pub. The publican thought the cigs were for myself and he gave me a lecture on saving my money and how he had saved up all his tuppences and how when he had grown up, he had been able to buy a public house. There was a sign hanging on the wall which said:

'All language allowed here
except bad language.'

When I came out, George roared to know what the hell had kept me. I told him the story of how the publican had bought his pub.

'He did in me eye,' said George. 'Go in and tell him that I said when he was a curate he put the price of every third pint in his own pocket'.

The rain was still falling hard and it looked as if it was down for the day. We passed the church on the hill and turned left at the top and went down the narrow side roads, emerging at Younge's crossroad garage. A few calls were made in between and then we headed for O'Gorman's cottage and Backweston, Leogh's and Kennedy's — the latter had at that time (in the war years) one aeroplane in a shed and the cocks and hens were playing pilots and air hostesses up and down the plane.

We journeyed back to Younge's and got the can boiled in Mrs. Reddy's house at Celbridge Abbey. We had our 'drum-up' (lunch) in the shelter of the trees in the driveway. After lunch, we headed for Celbridge and made a few calls in the White City, Salmon's pub, the fruit and sweet shop opposite, and crossed the bridge into Celbridge Town. Here we made many calls: the Mills, the Rectory, the house used by Dean Swift and Vanessa, Kane's shop, the Garda station and the parish priest's house, also Mr. Pursur's at the gate lodge and up the pebble-stone driveway to Castletown House, the largest house in Ireland.

George showed me the window which was boarded up and told me that the Devil had appeared in that room. Spence's paint mills were next on the route — they too, were very friendly and nice. Mrs. Spence always gave me sixpence or, sometimes, a shilling, for myself. Very few of the customers gave tips except at Christmas time but the Spence's never failed to have the sixpenny piece or shilling separate from the laundry money.

The van rolled back to the Hazelhatch Bridge where we called to Ruttle's stables. Mr. Ruttle trained *Workman,* a horse which won the Grand National. He offered me a job and said I'd make a very good jockey, but I decided to stay with my laundry parcels and Dublin streets, and I didn't fancy the idea of leaving Ma.

Next was Peamount Sanatorium to Mr. Clinton's house: he was a gentleman and he told me many things about horses and wild woodbine flowers. He treated me like a friend. He used wear a Robin Hood type hat, years and years before they became fashionable in Ireland.

An odd stop here and there and on to the Baldonnell Road, Mangans of Castledermot House and Baldonnell Aerodrome: the soldiers were very decent and never failed to bring me to the kitchen for a mug of tea, a few sausages, an egg or hot buttered scones. George and Tiny delivered to all the officers' houses, but I always went to the apprentices' quarters. Their laundry bills were very small — ninepence or a shilling at the most — mainly for a shirt and tie. At Christmas they made a collection for me and even collected from soldiers who were not customers. As a tired, cold, wet and hungry child I loved that kitchen in Baldonnell.

A few more stops and soon I saw the Round Tower of Clondalkin. Then Healy's pub, the butcher's shop, the Monastery Road, the Red Cow Inn, Fox and Geese and the white thatched cottage at the top of the Long Mile Road. Then delivery and collection of laundry was finished. Both sides of the Long Mile Road were wide-open fields down as far as the Halfway House and Drimnagh Castle. In summer, this was a lovers' lane area: but, on that wet, windy and dark September night, it was deserted. As we came down the Crumlin Road we met the crowd coming from the local Rialto and Leinster Cinemas. It was just eleven p.m. and the groups of boys and girls shouted at us: 'Hey, Mack, hey, Mack. Is this your half-day?'

Over and over again it was roared out: 'Yis are very early finishing. Is it yer half-day?'

I was too numb with the cold and wet even to try to answer. I just made the last bus home. The Ma cried again. I was wet to the skin and she wasn't too pleased about my having eaten the Free State army's food. Then, having thought it over she said it was okay. I could eat it if I was hungry.

I told her about the publican and saving money and she laughed. I had my dinner and we sat at the range fire and I told her all my stories and the offer of a job as a jockey. I turned over a chair, pretending it was a horse and Ma laughed again and again.

'Glory be to God!' she said, 'It's one o'clock. What time have you to be in at, in the morning?'

'Don't worry,' I said. 'Tomorrow is Thursday and I start at ten a.m. We finish about nine p.m. and Friday is my half-day. I'm in at seven-thirty a.m. on Saturday and Tiny said we finish about six o'clock. Friday is payday: fourteen shillings and sixpence. 'The rent,' I said, 'is almost twelve shillings and I'm paying it every week from now on.'

Ma put her arm around my shoulder and as we climbed the stairs we both sang together...

'All around my hat I wear a tri-coloured ribbon-o'.